ALAN BROWN

MODERN POLITICAL PHILOSOPHY

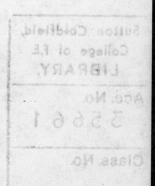

PENGUIN BOOKS

PENGUIN BOOKS

Published by the Penguin Group
Penguin Books Ltd, 27 Wrights Lane, London W8 5TZ, England
Viking Penguin, a division of Penguin Books USA Inc.
375 Hudson Street, New York, New York 10014, USA
Penguin Books Australia Ltd, Ringwood, Victoria, Australia
Penguin Books Canada Ltd, 2801 John Street, Markham, Ontario, Canada L3R 1B4
Penguin Books (NZ) Ltd, 182–190 Wairau Road, Auckland 10, New Zealand

Penguin Books Ltd, Registered Offices: Harmondsworth, Middlesex, England

First published in Pelican Books 1986
Reprinted in Penguin Books 1990
10 9 8 7 6 5 4 3 2

Printed in England by Clays Ltd, St Ives plc
Filmset in Monophoto Imprint

FOR MY MOTHER AND FATHER

CONTENTS

7

PREFACE

Political philosophy is once again thriving. That it was moribund for much of this century is a historical curiosity with which we need not here be overly concerned. It had to do with the dominance (at least in Anglophone countries) of a certain conception of philosophy, first as positivism and then as linguistic analysis, that is, thankfully, no longer in vogue. In fact, in dismissing political philosophy as largely confused or meaningless, this kind of philosophy signalled its own inadequacy.

The central questions of political philosophy concern the nature of the good or just society. Although practically significant – not to say crucial – this concern is not straightforward, for it is not at all obvious how to deal with it. In the chapters that follow I examine five major attempts to deal with political philosophy in a constructive manner. The first is the utilitarian system, a system which – it is fair to say – has been dominant, though not unchallenged, for over a century. I attempt to bring out the strengths and weaknesses of a theory which, despite constant attack, refuses to admit defeat. The second is the theory of John Rawls, whose book *A Theory of Justice* was the first substantially original effort in political philosophy for many a long year. Some would go so far as to say that this work is largely responsible for waking the discipline from its dogmatically induced slumbers. Indeed, Rawls's theory is best viewed as a reaction to utilitarianism, whereas our third approach, that of Robert Nozick, is certainly a complete departure. Here we encounter a nicely worked-out system based on the notion of certain human or moral rights, a system even more opposed to utilitarianism than that of Rawls. The fourth position to be considered is that of Marx. In the past decade or so this philosophy has been expressed with impressive intellectual rigour so that it can no longer be dismissed as merely left-wing rhetoric. The distinctive features of this approach are presented as leading on to the more adequate theory, that of neo-Aristotelianism. This, the last of the methods considered, is argued to be the correct approach to political philosophy both on the basis of the failures of its rivals and on its own merits. We have thereby completed a critical survey of the major political philosophies which should have provided some firm ground for political deliberations.

Thus in the final chapter we can consider some of the more general and important practical concerns of day-to-day politics. This all-too-brief discussion is intended more to indicate direction than demonstrate conclusions. Still, it does reveal the problems facing what is surely among the most complex of human concerns.

Thanks must be expressed, first, to Ted Honderich for the idea and the opportunity; second, to Lindsay Thomas and Perry Robertson for technical assistance; third, to Jim Harrison, whose politics are a constant source of inspiration; and finally, to all those who have ever tried to teach me philosophy, political or otherwise. Well may they tear their hair, gnash their teeth and wring their hands!

I.

INTRODUCTION

THE NATURE AND AIMS OF POLITICAL PHILOSOPHY

When men realized that they could act on the world and each other in a purposeful way – and it would seem that replacing instinct with rational inquiry was a historical event – they found themselves in a practical predicament. Reason told them that they had options but was less forthcoming about which option was best, or even about which considerations were relevant to the choice. It was obvious that there was a variety of possible ends, values or ideals which were relevant to how a man ought to live and act and how a community ought to organize. It was less obvious, on reflection, which of these values, if any, was correct.

Nor is it any more obvious today. In attempting to resolve these questions we engage in what we may call practical philosophy. The central question may be put thus: 'What is the best or right way for men to live, both as individuals and as a group?' On this basis we can distinguish two main branches of practical philosophy – ethics (or moral philosophy) and politics (more accurately political philosophy). Ethics is concerned with the individual: how ought he to live his life; what values and ideals ought he to adopt, what rules ought he to observe? Political philosophy is concerned with the social side of this question or, more precisely, with the problem of how society ought to be organized.

The central questions of political philosophy, then, somehow concern the nature of the good or right organization of society. This is not to beg any important questions about the nature of that philosophy itself, which is admittedly a contentious issue, for there are various ways in which we may concern ourselves with this question.

The first kind of concern is logical or analytical and focuses on the meaning and function of the concepts characteristic of practical discourse ('good', 'right', 'ought', 'must', etc.). What do we mean or imply when we state that something, say a society, is good or well-ordered, for example?

The second kind of concern is one of method. How do we determine what considerations are relevant, and in what way, in evaluating competing practical options? What kind of argument may we use? What kind of evidence may we appeal to? This concern will be examined in more detail in the next section.

The third concern we may call metaphysical. Here we inquire into the presuppositions of practical thought and discourse, and examine their consistency or otherwise with the presuppositions of our other ways of thinking (for example, in science or religion). We would hope that our procedures in these various spheres of human endeavour are at least consistent.

The fourth concern is that of application, that is, actually deciding on an option or policy. Deciding *how* to answer a question is not the same as answering it. Method has to be applied, theory converted into practice. Here we ask, and try to answer, the question: 'What actions or organizational forms are good or right?'

It should be noted that these concerns are not independent of one another. More specifically, answers to the later ones depend on the answers given to the earlier ones; for example, one cannot sensibly answer a question of substantive ethics (the fourth concern) unless one is aware of the meaning of the question and has some idea of what kind of support a correct answer requires.

On the other hand, it does seem possible to answer questions of meaning without relying on answers to our other questions. For this reason (though for others besides) philosophers in recent times have focused on questions of meaning; for this concern is in a sense purer, more abstract (a mode of thought which is philosophically attractive) and is, in this way, prior to any other.

Of course, there is danger in restricting ourselves to this question: if we do so our inquiries are in themselves pointless. For the whole point of asking such questions is to answer our practical concerns. An adequate practical philosophy must therefore push beyond questions of meaning to consider issues of method, metaphysics and application. Only then will the inquiry have served its function.

Of course a particular answer to the question of meaning may make later questions senseless or redundant, or answers to them trivial. For example, some philosophers think that when an ethical judgement is stated all that is being expressed, indeed all that could be expressed, are feelings, attitudes, decisions or commitments. Since this meaning commits us to ethical subjectivism – or scepticism about objective or true answers to ethical questions – our other concerns become trivial; questions of method reduce to concern over whether or not someone knows what he feels and whether or not they tell the truth about this; questions of metaphysics simply ask whether or not this psychology is a science and questions of application may be given the obvious answer.

Since I do not accept this view of the meaning of practical terms I do not accept that our other practical concerns are so trivial. In the course of discussing the major political philosophies of current interest I shall therefore touch on all of them. However, it is the second concern, the concern with method, which will occupy us for the most part. In this I follow the lead of John Rawls, whose major contribution to our subject is almost totally devoted to our second concern. Further, the question of method is more clearly the concern of the philosopher alone than is, say, the question of application. That question will concern the moralist, the priest, the politician, the writer of imaginative literature and so on. Again, the metaphysical questions, while philosophical, are not central to political inquiry. Still, the political philosopher will have to respond to all four questions if his inquiry is to be complete. These considerations should explain the particular emphasis adopted here.

Another way of fixing the nature of our inquiry more accurately is to consider the distinctions which define political science, political theory and political philosophy.

There is a well-worn distinction in philosophy which con-trasts description, explanation, a concern with causes and effects and so on, with evaluation or criticism and such like. Political science is concerned with the reality of political events (power struggles, voting trends, the relations between social class and party allegiance, etc.) and the explanatory theories dealing with them. Questions of value, or right and wrong in ethical terms, are left to one side in political science (or, at least, that is the ideal).

Since it is clear that questions of value must be considered there must be some discipline with this as its subject-matter. And this is frequently ascribed, indiscriminately, to political theory or political philosophy. However, there is a distinction to be observed here, as follows.

A political theory is a body of doctrine concerning a prefer-red organization of society, or aspects of it. Thus, for example, anarchism, liberalism and socialism are political theories. They are descriptions of candidates for the good or right society and comprise a plan or programme. Socialism, for example, may be conceived roughly as that form of society based on equality, community and rational planning. In our terms a political theory is a straightforward answer to our fourth concern, that of application. Such theories are often called 'ideologies' but I shall not be using the term in this sense as it is a technical term in Marxist thought, bringing in notions of how such theories are generated and sustained in society as well as ascribing to them a particular social function. It will be an open question, with the usage adopted here, whether or not a particular political theory is, at a particular time, ideological in nature.

Political philosophy is to be distinguished by its concern that such normative doctrines should be given philosophical grounds. That is to say, a political theory may or may not be rationally grounded. It may, for instance, be a simple rationaliza-tion of present practices or it may be taken on trust from some 'authority' like a religion. Political philosophy, on the other hand, will focus on how such doctrines may be properly justified. It is the inquiry into how the values, ideals, principles and so on which inform such theories are to be given rational grounds.

This in turn gives us another reason for emphasizing the

concern of method in our political philosophy, for other practical political concerns are more central to political science and theory.

Before going on to consider what method of inquiry is appropriate to political philosophy, however, it will be worth our while to consider in more detail the object of the inquiry. For clearly our choice of method will depend on the object or function which we ascribe to political philosophy. We must have a good idea of the proper object of our endeavours if we are to choose wisely amongst proposed methods. We already have some idea of this object from the above discussion, but there is a deal of controversy here which will repay examination.

Broadly, there seem to be three conceptions of the proper object of political philosophy. The first is the project of conceptual analysis. The second is the attempt to engage in piecemeal normative inquiry. The third is the project of developing a systematic, all-embracing practical philosophy of politics. This last is the object of the theories examined hereinafter, so it is well to be aware that the approach is not universal, and that its presuppositions are open to question.

Traditionally conceived, political philosophy concerns itself with certain perennial problems involving the nature of justice, political obligations and, more generally, the good society. The political philosopher ultimately prescribes some principle of justice or some form of government. The view of political philosophy as analysis, however – whatever that analysis is held to comprise – denies that the political philosopher can properly move from mere analysis (which is always presupposed anyway) to prescription.

One reason for this denial is the view that philosophy generally is analytic, a view which sees the grand questions of philosophy – the meaning of life, the nature of reality and our knowledge of it and so on – as either meaningless or confused. A proper conceptual analysis not only exhausts the field of legitimate inquiry but provides any answers it would be worth having. Or so it may be thought. But as we have seen, this approach answers only one of our legitimate concerns. Conceptual analysis cannot exhaust political philosophy. It is merely the application of a restricted method to the concepts of political theory, a method which is inadequate to the task in hand. No one doing political philosophy limits himself in this way, as a matter of fact, for there is always a suppressed normative content in such inquiries. In any event we must go further in order to answer our other concerns.

Current practice of a fuller conception of political philosophy diverges, however. On the one hand, there is an issue-by-issue or concept-by-concept approach in which a concept like democracy is put forward as a value (or, uncommonly, a disvalue). On the other, there is a full-blown, systematic approach in which nothing less than the principles and values (with their rankings) which ought to underlie society are revealed.

The flaw in practising political philosophy in the former way, that is in restricting it to some piecemeal tinkerings with our normative concepts, is that this approach actually presupposes the fuller, systematic conception if it is to make any sense. In effect, I venture, all properly conceived political philosophy tends, at the limit, to systematic political philosophy. That is, once all its presuppositions and implications are made explicit then its systematic character will be revealed. Thus both conceptual analysis and the partial concerns of piecemeal investigation must be seen as inadequate, considered by themselves, to the tasks of political philosophy.

Before discussing why this is so, however, it is necessary to say something more about what is meant by 'systematic'. In the traditional or grand style of political philosophy from Plato onwards, the aim was to describe and justify the values underlying a whole political system. Just as the preferred political and social system forms a more or less coherent whole so too does the political philosophy which underlies it. Or, at least, that is the intention.

We can begin with a common-sense idea. In order to engage in constructive political thought or criticism we need to enlarge our horizons beyond immediate concerns. For to implement sensible policy concerning, say, education, one must consider and deal with its implications in other areas, like taxation. In other words, a government requires a coherent programme of policy. This requires a comprehensive theory, a political theory, which in its turn requires a systematic political philosophy for its ground. Now such a perspective is unavailable on the basis of conceptual analysis or normative tinkering. They are inadequate because they are blind to the need for a full vision of the good society.

Thus we can see that to engage in politics one must accept the need for a political theory and to engage in political philosophy one must accept the comprehensive and systematic nature of the inquiry. There is at least an implicit requirement to engage with the totality of a political image, and, while we may on occasion merely discuss aspects of it, we are surely committed to saying that this part should be consistent with the rest, that our limited inquiry is of necessity comparative and relational. The truth, in other words, lies with the whole.

For this reason, piecemeal normative inquiries must be seen as illusory. If we are to argue, for instance, that freedom or equality are important values, we must say how important and compared to what; otherwise we have said little. At the limit we would wish to say how these values manifest themselves concretely in a coherent whole in some political theory. Of course such an approach is not without its problems and we shall examine some of these in later chapters. For now we need only recognize that systematic political philosophy and theory is the ideal of rationality in practical affairs.

This general, systematic, all-embracing approach may raise some fears at the very outset, however, for it raises the spectre of totalitarianism. In reply I think it must be accepted that this merely reflects reality. Politics does, in a sense, govern every aspect of our lives – for even those things left to the private concern of individuals are, as it were, conceded by the political realm. This was clearly observed by Aristotle, who identified the object of our practical inquiries as the good life for man and proposed politics as the science of that good,

> **... for it is this that ordains which of the sciences should be studied in the state, and which class of citizen should learn and up to what point they should learn them; and we see even the most esteemed of capacities to fall under this, e.g. strategy, economics, rhetoric; now since politics uses the rest of the sciences, and since, again, it legislates as to what we are to do and what we are to abstain from,**

the end of this science must include those of the others, so that this end must be the good for man.[1]

The importance of political thought to our lives is therefore difficult to overestimate. Governments, and social institutions generally, may determine more or less of an individual's life, and may be more or less coercive. The proper level of this control is a matter for investigation. The point to note, however, is that practical reasoning will be blinkered unless we take into account the possibilities and limitations which an examination of the political dimension of life may reveal.

The need for political philosophy is therefore linked to the Socratic project of examining one's life. It may be going too far to say that the unexamined life is not worth living, but if reason and wisdom have any value then such a life will be less than satisfactory. And to ignore the political dimension of life is to adopt a position which is inadequate in practice. Political inquiry may thus be understood as the completion of our project of practical reasoning, the search for practical wisdom.

METHOD IN POLITICAL PHILOSOPHY

Political philosophy is concerned with the meaning, source and force of values. In emphasizing the question of method in political philosophy, we place questions of moral knowledge in a central position. And it is with reference to this concern that we must attempt to assess the principles and values that underpin a view of the good or right society.

The question of method may best be approached via a consideration of the kind of knowledge or theory our political philosophy is to offer. There are several candidates for this.

First, practical philosophy may be viewed as a form of inquiry like that of natural science. For example, utilitarianism (the theory that things are to be justified in terms of their contribution to the production of 'utility') can be presented as an inductive inference (inference to the best general principle) from common moral experience, that is, our beliefs and judgements. This would parallel the generality of a notion like, say, gravity, which makes general sense of our experience of falling bodies. But such a comparison seems superficial, since the raw data involved are of different orders. As Hume observed, moral opinion seems to be an imposition on human affairs by us; it is human thought that brings value into the world. Bodies, on the other hand, fall regardless. Another attempt to hold on to this view is associated with 'moral-sense' theory. This holds that human beings are possessed of a moral sense, like our other senses, which enables us to perceive moral aspects of reality – and those aspects are just as real as the falling of bodies. This, it seems to me, is not a likely story.

A second comparison to be considered is that of mathematics, or parts thereof. On one view of these matters a discipline like geometry consists of deductive inferences from a set of axioms which boast the property of self-evidence. However, though some may claim to have discovered moral or practical axioms of this nature, the approach is not promising. What appears self-evident to some seems problematic, or even false, to others.

A third way of conceiving moral belief would be to compare it with religious belief, where that is understood to be a matter of faith. On such a view we are to take a moral or practical code (though which one?) to be justified, not by reason or observation, but by the act of faith which leads one to embrace it. How such a leap of faith may be said to justify anything is something of a mystery – but that seems here to be accepted as the nature of things.

More generally we can distinguish two approaches which make practical knowledge accessible to reason: the *a priori* and the *a posteriori*.

To see practical knowledge as *a priori* is to see it as knowledge we cannot learn from experience, so that, for example, knowledge of values may be generated from pure reason or may be directly intuited. On the other hand, to see practical knowledge as *a posteriori* is to see it as something we have to learn from experience. For example, some hold that values are products of a vision of the good life for man, a vision based on a theory of human nature. And we know about human nature by studying it.

Of course there is an alternative to all or any of these attempts to gain practical knowledge, and that is to deny that we can have any such knowledge. Scepticism about the possibility of practical knowledge has a distinguished philosophical tradition.

But we must be careful to distinguish two types of scepticism. The first relates to practical thought generally and claims that values, ideals, principles and so on lack any objective basis. Ultimately, they are matters for choice, commitment or perhaps indoctrination. That is all the status that they can have. The second relates specifically to *moral values*. On this view it is possible to justify a practical position only if that position is not a moral one. By 'moral' here is meant concern for the welfare of people in general or respect for duties or obligations which tend to the same object. An example of moral scepticism would be ethical egoism, the view that an individual is justified in pursuing only his own interests.

If this range of views about the nature or possibility of knowledge of values seems complex, then what follows may seem bewildering – though since the following chapters are devoted to dispelling this it is hoped that bewilderment will be short-lived.

The question of method, in our sense, comes to this: what considerations are relevant, and to what extent, in the determination of how society ought to be organized? Just as a method of ethics, to use Sidgwick's term,[2] is a view about the manner in which an individual is to determine what he ultimately ought to do or be, so a method of politics, or political philosophy, is a view about what considerations are relevant, and how, to the question of how society ought to be organized.

The history of political philosophy is littered with suggestions. At various times, in various places, it has been argued that we attend to some system of *human rights*, the outcome of a process begun in some *state of nature*, the agreement attendant upon some *social contract*, the structure resulting from the systematization of *ordinary moral opinion*, and the judgement of some *ideal observer*. Of course, these are not the only contenders for the title of the grounds of political right. But they are the main ones, having recurred from time to time or endured longer than most. In fact, they persist in some form or other in current thought. In later chapters we shall be examining the use of these devices and their presuppositions about the nature and possibility of moral knowledge in order to assess the proposed grounds of political philosophy.

In general, we may subject these grounds to two forms

of criticism, the one internal, the other external. The internal criticism examines the logic of the argument as presented. It is a test for coherence. For example, it is sometimes objected to Rawls's theory[3] that his conclusion (his 'principles of justice') does not follow from the grounds which he offers. This ground, the 'original position', tends instead, it is argued, to support the principle of utility, something which Rawls explicitly rejects.

The external form of criticism goes deeper. Instead of accepting the grounds of the theory and examining the argument from it, the external assessment examines what reasons there may be for accepting the grounds themselves. To take the example of Rawls again, Ronald Dworkin offers this piece of external assessment:

> **The device of the original position ... cannot plausibly be taken as the starting point for political philosophy. It requires a deeper theory beneath it, a theory that explains why the original position has the features that it does and why the fact that people would choose particular principles in that position, if they would, certifies those principles as principles of justice.[4]**

The main focus of attention, then, in an inquiry into the method of political philosophy should be on how a topic is introduced or how a problem is set up. There, if anywhere, must lie the power of the resultant structure. It is to this basic move – the setting up of a starting point or frame of reference – that a methodological study in political philosophy must address itself. Of course few political philosophers have reflected on method very explicitly or as a preliminary to their main work, but the viability of their method is the ultimate target for criticism as well as the central pillar of supposed support. To choose to begin one's theorizing using human rights or the state of nature, for example, as one's frame of reference is to invite questions as to why. They are not obviously correct starting points.

Nozick, in an attack on the notion that justice demands equality,[5] reveals an awareness of such considerations, asking why equality should be 'the rest position of the system, deviation from which may be caused only by moral forces?' This plurality of at least plausible starting points highlights the need for an adequate methodological framework. We must find some way of discovering which, if any, of our candidates is the correct one.

In what follows we will meet the current favourites, none of them essentially new. The intention of the foregoing has been to equip us with some essential tools for the task of assessing various political philosophies. The questions raised and the distinctions introduced have given us at least some criteria for recognizing success and failure in the process of practical philosophy.

2.

UTILITARIANISM
AND THE TELEOLOGY OF WELFARE

Utilitarianism is a well-established practical philosophy. It forms the point of departure even for much theory which fundamentally rejects it. In trying to assess the theory, however, we soon discover that there is more than one theory calling itself utilitarian, so that we must begin by distinguishing the varieties on offer. There is, though, a vocabulary and, more importantly, a structure common to this genus of practical philosophy. As a political philosophy utilitarianism enjoins that we prefer and try to bring about that form of social and political organization which produces *the greatest amount of utility*.

More broadly, utilitarianism is a theory which attempts to evaluate any solution to a practical issue in terms of a certain aspect of the *consequences* of that solution. That aspect of the consequences which is held to matter is called *utility* and this is conceived to be the sole or fundamental value. It is this that gives value or point to everything we do and anything else can only have *instrumental* value; everything has value only in so far as it promotes utility. Because utility is this ultimate good the utilitarian naturally prefers more of it to less in all circumstances, hence the utilitarian injunction to maximize utility.

Utilitarianism is thus a species of consequentialism, the doctrine that what matters, in the final analysis, is some feature of the consequences of an act or social system. This may be contrasted with assessment based on the *rightness* of an act or system (which some think matters regardless of the consequences). In rejecting this latter view, the 'deontological' view, consequentialism is ascribing priority to 'the good' (the consequences' value) over 'the right'. This means that justice, or whatever, must be *derived* from the principles which concern the good. Thus utilitarianism will allow for such rules only if they help to maximize utility. Utilitarianism is therefore to be distinguished from other consequentialist theories by its particular construal of value (as utility) and by its demand to maximize the good (there could be lesser demands: for instance, merely to prohibit what is bad or ensure that a set level of good is achieved).

THE VARIETIES OF UTILITARIANISM

Since utilitarianism is characterized by a maximizing principle, the source of variation in the theory stems from differences in opinion concerning the nature of utility. There are three main schools of thought here. The first is the *classical* school, originating with Bentham, which interprets utility hedonistically – that is, as pleasure. The sole ultimate good is the experience of this mental state; all else has value as it contributes to this. The second variety is called *preference* or welfare utilitarianism, which stems from modern welfare economics. The thing to be maximized here (the 'maximand') is not pleasure, but the satisfaction of wants or desires as revealed in actual or predicted preferences. The third version is called *ideal* utilitarianism. This form allows that other things may be ultimate goods, that not everything has value only as it contributes to maximizing pleasure. Moore, for example, identifies personal relations and aesthetic experiences as such goods.[1]

Several areas are proposed for the application of utilitarian evaluation. Bentham himself generalized his theory into a comprehensive practical philosophy so that in our evaluation of all practical affairs (and this includes individual actions, character dispositions, social policies and social structures) the real object of concern ought to be the consequences in terms of utility for all those affected.

Generally, however, we can distinguish three areas of possible application for utilitarianism which, on the face of it, need not be run together.

First, there is the sphere of personal choice or ethics. In determining what in life it is best to be or do, the ethical utilitarian makes it clear what we must *do*: maximize utility. However, it seems less clear what it is best to *be*. On the one hand, it is best to be a utility maximizer (simply as a consequence of what it is best to do), while on the other it seems best to *experience* as much utility as possible (because the experience of utility is the ultimate good). These two approaches to utility, the egoistic and the universal, create great strain in ethical utilitarianism – as we shall see later when we examine the grounds of the theory. Ethical utilitarianism faces other problems, such as whether the individual pursuit of utility ('act' utilitarianism) produces the greatest total. Some think it better that we should observe rules of conduct which coordinate our activities so as to maximize utility ('rule' utilitarianism). Again it may be wondered whether actually *being* a utilitarian is a 'healthy' form of living: would it not destroy any prospect of a truly good life, sacrificing one's 'integrity', one's friends, indeed one's 'morality' on the altar of utility?

The second area of application is the area of public or social policy formation – the taking of decisions about taxation, defence, the environment, and so on. Whoever makes these decisions is advised to use the utilitarian principle. Areas of concern here include whether to so do may violate democratic decision procedures or the rights of those affected.

The third area of possible application is in the evaluation of whole social structures. In evaluating competing theories of the well-ordered society the utilitarian will recommend that system which produces the most utility. It is at this level of generality that utilitarianism presents itself as a political philosophy. Obviously there will be a tendency to accept or reject the utilitarian principle in all three areas so that for those who reject utilitarianism as an ethical theory it will not seem worthwhile to consider its merits as a political philosophy. However, this is not something that may be taken for granted.

Consider, in this context, the analogy of a zoo. Say we accept that zoos have an ultimate end or good which a good zoo will attempt to maximize; and say, for the sake of argument, that this end is to entertain their human visitors. No one requires that the animals should share this end (even if they could) or, less obviously, that the keepers must run the zoo *as* a place of entertainment. For it may be that to produce most entertainment we should view animals in the natural state and not as part of a circus act.

Having examined where the utilitarian principle may be applied we now consider how. Few utilitarians have been content with the simple injunction to maximize utility. While simply stated this demand may appear over-abstract, making it difficult to see what would satisfy it. Accordingly, utilitarians have traditionally offered more concrete equivalents and clarifications. Let us consider a few.

The first of these prompts us to promote the greatest happiness of the greatest number. This formula was initially endorsed by Bentham, but later rejected, because we can maximize the happiness of the greatest number (a simple majority) while at the same time decreasing the total amount of happiness. This would happen, for example, if just under half a population were turned into slaves for the remaining majority. This majority might have its happiness maximized but the aggregate of happiness would decrease if, as seems likely, the misery of the slaves outweighed the increase in happiness for the masters.

The second formula tells us that each is to count for one, no one for more than one. From the utilitarian point of view the pleasure of a lord is no more desirable than that of a common worker. Who experiences the pleasure does not affect the value of the pleasure. This seems fair enough. However, the formula also imposes constraints which look to be irrational on utilitarian grounds. Consider the difference in efficiency in the conversion of resources into happiness by the naturally miserable, the spoilt child and the person obsessed with some expensive ambition. The utilitarian should be inclined to distribute resources where they will be most efficiently used, since this will tend to maximize utility. Accordingly, the apparent equality of this second formula is at best superficial. It would be better expressed by saying that a man's station does not directly affect the value of his pleasures. Utilitarians cannot avoid saying that the pleasure of an evil man in itself counts as much as that of a good man, since who is happy is, in itself, irrelevant. We still have to accept the utilitarian idea that the only basis on which to value a good man's pleasure more is that a society of good men will be a happier place than a society of bad men. Bad men are therefore to be discouraged.

The third issue of formulation concerns the problem of whose happiness is to be considered. We have to establish the range of application of the principles (whose happiness counts) if we are to formulate plans for its promotion. Bentham, who was given to great variety in his formulations, described the principle of utility as a principle which approves or disapproves of every action according to the tendency which it appears to have to augment or diminish the happiness of the party whose interest is in question. Rawls, a modern critic, ascribes to utilitarianism the view 'that society is rightly ordered, and therefore just, when its major institutions are arranged so as to achieve the greatest net balance of satisfaction summed over all the individuals belonging to it.'[2] These two approaches equate with each other only when a society's *members* are seen as comprising all the parties whose interests are in question.

However, this equation seems unsatisfactory from the utilitarian point of view. Consider a society which organized itself so as to be a military threat to its neighbours. Using this threat it could exploit its neighbours to provide cheap or free resources (both raw materials and labour) and thus give itself an easy lifestyle. It would be a happier society than otherwise. We would not be disposed to think highly of it, however, nor should the utilitarian. For he surely has no ground for treating members of a particular society (even if it is his own) as the only ones who count. On the other hand, the utilitarian cannot treat of societies in isolation, for he cannot ignore the contribution one society could make to the welfare of another. Thus, according to some utilitarians, our society (any rich society) should organize so as to maximize its foreign-aid programme – for it is amongst the world's poor that the greatest increase in utility can be made for a given amount of resources. A similar consideration urged on utilitarian calculation concerns the welfare of non-human animals. Because animals are capable of experiencing pleasure and pain some utilitarians argue that we cannot ignore their welfare; in particular that using animals as food, pets and entertainment is just another form of exploitation (across species rather than societies) which cannot be countenanced.

We must accept, then, that utility is to be maximized and that no one (or kind) is to be privileged save on grounds of efficiency. And here animals may score over humans – they can be more easily made happy. Some may conclude therefore that humanity should commit collective suicide on utilitarian grounds.

The fourth problem over formulation is the issue of whether *average* or *total* utility should be what we maximize. Total utility is calculated simply by summing the net amounts of happiness enjoyed by each individual. Average utility is this total divided by the number of individuals concerned. It is often observed, correctly, that the two versions always coincide in output except when the issues concern whether certain people ought to exist (now or in the future).

However, an examination of this divergence may be illuminating. The first thing to note is that we may be able to increase the total amount of utility while lowering the average level of that utility by increasing the population. This would be so if the resources now used to maintain a high average could be more efficiently deployed to create utility for new people. Similarly we may be able to raise the average level of utility and lower the total by decreasing the size of the population. This would be so if those large numbers of people who consume next to nothing as individuals, but substantial amounts collectively, could be made to disappear, and the resources redirected to the more fortunate remaining minority. Thus whether one is an advocate of the maximizing of average or total utility will affect the way one approaches certain of the world's problems. The average utilitarian is more likely to advocate keeping the population to a minimum ratio with resources. The aggregate utilitarian will want to increase the population size so long as utility increases also. I leave the reader to ponder on the appeal of these alternatives. But it must be said that from the utilitarian point of view which identifies happiness as the sole good, average utilitarianism looks to be irrational. For why pursue something which can result in lessening the amount of what has value?

In general, then, it is best and clearest to conceive utilitarianism as the injunction to maximize utility and to conceive political utilitarianism as the injunction to order society so as to maximize utility. Before we can assess this doctrine properly, however, we have to reduce the variety still further. Having isolated the maximizing principle as the best characterization of the structure of utilitarianism, we must now decide which is the best account of its content. Does classical, preference or ideal utilitarianism offer the best maximand? Each theory has its problems but for several reasons I want to argue that both preference and ideal utilitarianism are non-starters. In essence, preference utilitarianism takes as its maximand something we could not seriously accept as the sole ultimate value and while ideal utilitarianism offers a more plausible account of ultimate values these are not something we can sensibly maximize. But let me explain.

The classical theory is frequently attacked on the technical grounds that it requires us to identify and measure occurrences of pleasure (a private mental state) as well as determine what causes them. This, it is argued, is hopelessly complex. In particular, the problems of measurement are stressed.

First, it may be thought of as a conceptual problem whether the concept of pleasure really corresponds to something substantial, as the utilitarian requires. Of course, no one seriously doubts the existence of pleasure. The real doubt is whether it is the sort of thing the utilitarian wants and needs it to be, a simple homogeneous psychological state or experience which accompanies all the activities people call enjoyable. This may seem unlikely, however, since the psychological pay-off from some enjoyable activities is pain – we may, for example, enjoy painful physical exercise.

The utilitarian may respond to this in two ways. First, he can argue that these unpleasant activities are only valued for their further pleasurable effects – in the above example the pleasures of being fit, the sense of achievement and superiority. The utilitarian will argue that if these goods can be achieved painlessly (through the use of drugs, for example) then this is clearly preferable. And it would seem he has a point. Second, he can simply call whatever we find worthwhile pleasant. But apart from being an implausible definition, this means that pleasure is not a simple single thing – and hence is useless in utilitarian calculation.

This same difficulty emerges again in the second set of problems facing the measurement of pleasure – those of epistemology. For even if pleasure is a simple homogeneous entity accompanying everything we could reasonably call worthwhile, can we really know, in comparing two experiences, which is the more pleasant? Even if pleasure, defined independently of what we find worthwhile, is or ought to be the common measure of value underlying the very considerable diversity in the things people find worthwhile, can we really compare the pleasures of eating good food, driving fast cars, scoring the winning goal, bringing up a baby, etc., etc.? Worse, can we know that someone enjoyed some event more (and by how much) than some *other* person?

These are the problems of commensurability and interpersonal comparison, of converting everyone's pleasures into a common currency – giving them a 'price'. Utilitarianism of any sort requires this kind of conversion. Using the techniques of welfare economics, preference utilitarianism attempts to do just this. This is not the place to probe the intricacies of the economic theory, however. If the theory succeeds it will measure the *intensities* of an individual's preferences (thus formulating his *'utility function'*) and be able to *compare* the intensities of preference for different individuals. In my view preference utilitarianism will do little better than the classical theory in these respects, though within its own assumptions it may be able to generate fairly complex and precise calculations. The main problem with the theory is that it adopts subjective preference as the basis for evaluation. The satisfaction of a preference is an unacceptable object of ultimate concern. How could anyone think that this has value in itself? Remember we are not speaking of satisfaction as such (which *may* be thought of as good in itself), but the satisfaction of a desire or preference. The satisfaction of a desire only contingently results in satisfaction itself, since getting what we want does not always please us.

It really makes no sense to treat an individual's preference satisfaction as what ultimately matters, since it clearly makes sense to say that people have interests which the satisfaction of their desires only sometimes promotes. The preference utilitarian is giving preferences a status which they do not deserve; he does not care how preferences arise or whether their satisfaction will actually benefit people.

Similarly, it seems impossible to see the satisfaction of preferences as good in itself when people may have preferences for the abhorrent – for instance, the suffering of others. It may be thought that the classical theory shares this problem, since people may take pleasure in the suffering of others. In accepting that pleasure is good in itself, Bentham, for example, accepted that it is better (*ceteris paribus*) if a murderer *enjoys* killing. But there is a difference here. At least the classical theory is locating value in something positive, in something that can plausibly be called good if we can consider it in isolation from its source. What possible value could there be in satisfying a desire to murder (remembering that this is not the same as satisfying the murderer)?

To save the theory from this kind of criticism, some preference utilitarians accept the need for some way of filtering out such unsavoury preferences. It may be suggested that we count only 'rational' preferences, for example. Dworkin has suggested that we count only 'internal' preferences (those concerned with benefits to the person expressing the preference); 'external' preferences (those concerned with the benefits to others) are to be ignored.[3]

Perhaps there are ways of arriving at a set of preferences which are more deserving of consideration. But clearly they do not help to show that preference satisfaction is good in itself. In fact they support the opposite view. If only certain preferences are to count, then it cannot be preferences *as such* which count, and it is difficult to avoid the conclusion that those preferences which do count do so in virtue of the consequences of satisfying them.

It seems clear, then, that preference utilitarianism has great difficulty in attempting to present desire satisfaction as an ultimate value. From a utilitarian point of view, the defects of this maximand must outweigh its attractions. Can the theory, perhaps, be treated as a practical approximation to the classical theory, welding the hedonistic theory of the good and the calculating power of economic theory? This seems highly unlikely. It would only be so if choices were rationally (if not intentionally) directed towards the production of utility (that is, pleasure). Adam Smith, for one, thought that this was the case in a free market economy, where the invisible hand guided the whole to utility. However, even if this is so (and many disagree) the economy is but one area of life. In other areas people have many 'irrational' preferences (for example, those based on moral, political or religious beliefs), the satisfaction of which would tend not to maximize utility (or pleasure), and which must therefore be ignored. In so doing the utilitarian is relying on his original concern for maximizing pleasure.

There are, of course, many alternative grounds for valuing a person's choices – for instance, that to do so respects his autonomy, that freedom is a great value in itself or that people have a right to such respect. This, however, is to move away from utilitarianism entirely – for these amount to competing moral systems.

As mentioned before, ideal utilitarianism takes as its maximand not a single value but a range of them, a set of things considered good in themselves. In accepting a diversity of basically good things, however, the theory ceases to be utilitarian. Although the theory remains consequentialist in that things are to be evaluated with respect to the goodness of their consequences, the injunction to maximize goodness (utility) can no longer be applied. This is because the basic calculating mentality of utilitarianism is inappropriate. If there is a diversity of basically good things, that in virtue of which they are good will not be a single comparable and measurable entity. Thus when forced to choose between creating one good or an alternative (say pleasure or aesthetic experience) we cannot reduce these to a common scale and choose which is greater.

That, indeed, is the main point of deriving all value from a single source. If we deny this source, then we must accept that the injunction to maximize makes little sense. Similarly, another major motive for the utilitarian project is lost if we adopt the ideal variety. Utilitarianism is meant to *explain* the value of everything by showing that its consequences are pleasant. But in accepting other basic goods we lose the point of this explanation; the value of all the basic goods has to be independently established – and for those who wish to include an aspect of morality (for instance, justice) among the basic goods this consequentialism just avoids the issue. The original utilitarians wanted to show that morality could be derived from the rational pursuit of the objective (non-moral) good of pleasure. I do not wish to suggest that this kind of theory is untenable – I shall examine the issues involved here in Chapter 6. However, it seems clear that the theory has little to do with utilitarianism proper and is best left aside.

We must conclude then that the classical theory is the strongest, although it faces grave computational problems. If we are to be utilitarians at all we must be classical ones. It seems best, therefore, to define utilitarianism as that form of consequentialism which is concerned simply to maximize goodness and that the utilitarian idea of goodness is simply pleasure. I turn now to attempts to justify this view of value theory.

THE GROUNDS OF UTILITARIANISM

The grounds of a political principle enjoining the maximization of utility is something utilitarians themselves dispute. In this section I want to inquire into the more commonly proposed grounds and into whether there are any compelling arguments for them.

The simplest form an argument for utilitarianism could take rests on the claim that utility (however conceived) is the sole ultimate value. Since it is always better to have more of a good thing than less (*ceteris paribus*) and because any constraint on the pursuit of the ultimate value must be derived from that value, we have to accept the rationality of maximizing utility. To put it another way, the truth of the claim that utility is the sole ultimate value ensures that the *ceteris paribus* condition always applies, that there is never any other consideration which is to be taken into account.

This argument encapsulates much of the appeal of utilitarianism, its apparent simplicity and coherence, its independence of mysterious moral absolutes and metaphysical origins, and its tough-minded rationality. Of course the apparent simplicity of the argument conceals a mass of assumption about the nature of morality and the proper method of procedure in moral argument. None the less, something like it occurs in most defences of utilitarianism and it is to the variety of such defences that I now turn.

We may begin with Bentham, whose great inspiration was the philosophy of Hume. Bentham borrowed the principle of utility from Hume, though he noted the main difference in their approach. Whereas Hume had sought to *explain* society's institutions by way of their utility, Bentham sought to *justify* his proposed reforms of society on the same grounds. What ought to be should conform to the principle. However, the break from Hume is not so clear cut as this suggests. For Bentham frequently advances the utility principle as a generalization from actual human behaviour, opining that men are governed by a hedonistic psychology (pursuing pleasure and shunning pain). All action, or all rational, sane action, is hedonistic.

How could we come to believe this? Perhaps a device of Hume would be helpful. In his discussion of practical reasoning Hume argues for the view that reason is the slave of the passions and, to demonstrate this, invites us to trace chains of practical reasoning back to their origin. The origin, Hume thinks, will always be a 'passion'. However, though the term passion may connote a hedonistic psychology, no one could be more insistent than Hume that desire is not just desire for pleasure. Bentham, on the other hand, opts for the less plausible view that all desires focus in the final analysis exclusively on pleasure or pain, and it is from this that his central argument for utilitarianism proceeds.

According to Bentham[4] the principle of utility cannot be

proven, for a proof must proceed either from observation (and a normative principle cannot be observed or derived logically from what can be observed) or from a deduction from a more general principle (and by definition there can be no more general principle). However, he did think it can be very strongly supported, and we can glean from his writings a version of the straightforward argument outlined above.

The first step is the claim that human nature is hedonistic. All we ever do is pursue pleasure and try to evade pain. This being so, only pleasure could occupy the role of the good, of the ultimate value. For Bentham, and naturalistic thought generally, it would be inconceivable that our necessary ends could be anything other than good. This line of thought can be traced back to Aristotle, for whom a thing's natural end (or *telos*) was also its good, 'for the good has rightly been declared to be that at which all things aim'. Aristotle, however, was not a hedonist.

The doctrine of psychological hedonism is at best implausible. Bentham thinks we cannot act other than to pursue pleasure and shun pain, that nature has placed mankind under the governance of these two sovereign masters. While we may prefer to think of ourselves as often motivated by higher (or, at any rate, more complex) concerns, this must be self-deception. Thus the hedonist is much concerned to reinterpret our behaviour in his own terms, explaining that our 'real' reasons for doing what we do (everything we do) centre on considerations of pleasure and pain. This pleasure is the good for man, like it or not (and of course we really must); it is nature's immutable prescription.

To many this has seemed unacceptable. To label other-motivated behaviour non-existent or pathological seems at best arbitrary. Far better to follow Hume, for example, and see pleasure as more often a byproduct of the successful pursuit of some other end than as always an end in itself. Indeed, as is often pointed out, the pursuit of pleasure is ill-served by seeking pleasure itself and best served by the pursuit of fulfilling projects whose success pleasure attends. Thus for nature to have placed us under these sovereign masters would have been a self-defeating strategy.

Of course to deny psychological hedonism is not to deny that pleasure is the ultimate human good (ethical hedonism). It does, however, block what seems to be the most direct route to that claim. In order to examine the rest of Bentham's argument we must grant that some other route is possible; that it is possible to show that pleasure is the good.

The second step in the argument is the familiar claim that since pleasure is the sole good it is of no direct consequence who experiences the pleasure except as this affects the total. Thus to pursue pleasure egoistically or with limited benevolence is irrational. It is irrational to treat particular individuals (including oneself) as irreducible or distinct objects of concern in our practical deliberations.

The third step, again familiar, is the claim that since pleasure is the sole good it is simply irrational not to prefer more to less, so that pleasure ought to be maximized.

Combining steps two and three we get the principle of utility: 'maximize pleasure'. We can get from hedonism to utilitarianism in successive reasonable steps. But I think we can see that the argument as a whole is unsuccessful for a variety of reasons.

In the first place, it does not follow from the fact that pleasure always features in our ends that pleasure as such is our aim (and hence our good). For it is impossible to observe that all people everywhere pursue pleasure in the reductive sense required (that is, reduced, or abstracted, from the other aspects of the ends necessarily involved). Even if pleasure is all that I pursue it is not possible to observe that I do so *as such* and hence that dissociated pleasure is the good. For what would be observed is that I always pursue the pleasure of assignable individuals (myself, my friends, the needy or whatever) and thus we could conclude only that the good is the pleasure of some person or persons and not pleasure as such. This restricted conclusion prevents the utilitarian result in the second step above since that requires the depersonalization of the pleasure pursued in our ends.

Similarly, the conclusion that everyone ought to pursue pleasure in general (utility) rests on the view that who feels the pleasure is irrelevant. But it is the experience of pleasure that is good (indeed pleasure can only be an experience) and I experience only my own pleasure, no one else's. It is unclear therefore how someone else's pleasure can be a good to me, since the experiencing of it is denied me.

Thus there is a deep problem for the hedonist in transcending egoism, at least if the argument for hedonism proceeds as Bentham's does.

Perhaps it would be replied that we can get to this pristine pleasure by observing that pleasure as such is the only common factor in our pleasure-ridden ends. But of course that is not enough, even if true, to force the conclusion that isolated pleasure is the ultimate value. For we require the stronger claim that dissociated pleasure is *all* that matters to us in our ends – and that is not an observable fact. In any case, it is not true that pleasure is the only common factor. For it would seem that we also always care who gets it. Similarly, even if pleasure were the only common factor in all the things we pursue, it still would not follow that pleasure is the sole good. For it could be that we have a variety of ultimate ends, each of which happens to include an element of pleasure.

Thus we can conclude that Bentham's derivation of the principle of utility fails. It begins with an implausible psychological hedonism and can get no further.

We can now turn to Bentham's successor in the history of utilitarian theory – J. S. Mill.[5] Mill begins in Benthamite vein, declaring that 'happiness is desirable, and the only thing desirable, as an end; all other things being desirable only as a means to that end'.[6] Further, by 'happiness, is intended pleasure, and the absence of pain; by unhappiness, pain and the privation of pleasure'.[7]

In his famous proof Mill is arguing to the conclusion that pleasure is *one* of the ends of conduct. By this he means that pleasure is a good in itself, an ultimate value. It is only later that he addresses the problem of how it can be shown to be the only ultimate good, as utilitarianism requires. His argument is complex and rather vague but proceeds as follows:

> **The sole evidence it is possible to produce that anything is desirable, is that people do actually desire it . . . Each person, so far as he believes it to be attainable, desires his own happiness . . . [Thus] happiness is good . . . , each person's happiness is a good to that person and the general**

happiness therefore, [is] a good to the aggregate of all persons.[8]

In order to make sense of this the following restatement may be helpful:

1. If something is ultimately desired (that is, not desired for the sake of something else or is a final end in a chain of practical reasoning) then it can be an end of conduct.

2. If something is an end of conduct then it is a good (to the person concerned).

3. Happiness (pleasure) is such an end – because each person ultimately desires it.

4. Happiness (pleasure) is therefore a good to its possessor.

5. Because pleasure is a good to everyone it is a good as such and the general happiness (aggregate of pleasure) ought to be an end of moral conduct.

Mill is trying to get to a weaker conclusion than that of Bentham (that the utility principle is at least one of the principles of morality) from a weaker premise (that pleasure is at least one of our ultimate ends). Mill is not relying here, then, on psychological hedonism. To say that 'each person desires his own happiness' is not to say that this is all that he desires. For the same reason we cannot claim that Mill is an egoist. The key moves in the argument, then, occur in the first and last of the five statements above. Let us look at each in turn.

In the first Mill is claiming that if something is really an ultimate end in practice then it must be an ultimately valuable thing. And this seems undeniable if we remember that this means valuable to the person concerned. The fact that each person desires his own happiness is all the proof we need that happiness is a good – (remembering still) to that person. So far so good.

The problem, however, is that we can still ask of the person whether pleasure (which he admittedly treats as good) really is good – whether he really ought to aim at pleasure as an ultimate end. Since what we seek is a normative principle (that which we ought to do is maximize pleasure) it seems necessary to begin from something like the claim that people ought to aim at pleasure (given the way Mill's argument proceeds). And remember Mill cannot rely on Bentham's claim that people have no choice but to pursue pleasure.

It is clear, then, that Mill thinks that what people actually desire and pursue in life has some bearing on what they ought to pursue, or what it is good for them to pursue. However, even if it is a fact that everyone to some extent behaves hedonistically (as might be expected in a materialistic and spiritually empty age) this seems a bad argument for the conclusion that this is a worthy or good way to live. It relies, first, on an unscientific, socially and historically biased observation of common behaviour. Second, it seems to ignore the common claim that one cannot derive conclusions about how things ought to be in a simple logical step from how things in fact are. More particularly, in actually having pleasure as an end we cannot thereby guarantee it as a good. Indeed, as noted earlier it may be a self-defeating end to adopt (and thus no good to itself). In fact, there are many ends we have which we know to be bad for us. Many of us smoke cigarettes, for example, and few of us used car seat-belts before the law required it. Are final ends somehow immune from this kind of error?

Of course Mill had reason to prefer that people should be allowed to live as they please, within certain limits (as he had argued earlier in his *On Liberty*[9]), and hence we can supply a motive for his wanting to declare the chosen life the good life. But that motive in no way justifies his simplistic naturalist move. In the first place one cannot allow one's political leanings (in this case liberalism) to influence one's moral epistemology so simply – especially when the argument is so bad. In the second, since Mill's defence of liberty in fact depends on his utilitarianism, such a manoeuvre would be viciously circular, justifying liberty by its utility and utility by the value of liberty in the choice of the good life.

There are, of course, other views of the good life which eschew pleasure entirely and Mill would simply have us ignore them when he moves on to argue that utility is the *only* end of conduct. He makes this seem plausible by labelling his good 'happiness'. In fact he means pleasure. Now in his ethics Aristotle had simply asserted that happiness is the good for man, knowing that no one could disagree. All men agree on this, not because they all pursue the same thing (there are many things men pursue – power, honour, wealth, pleasure and so on) but because they all call whatever they in fact desire and pursue by this name. Indeed it would be irrational to call it anything else. The substantive issue in ethics is to discover who, if anyone, is correct, but in equating happiness with pleasure Mill is merely begging the question in favour of his own preference.

Mill's first move is thus deeply problematic. Before examining what is involved in the final fifth step it is worth seeing how Mill tries to move from the argument that pleasure is one of the reasonable ends of conduct to the claim that it is the only such end. Ultimately, Mill follows Bentham in relying on psychological hedonism: 'to desire anything, except in proportion as the idea of it is pleasant, is a physical and metaphysical impossibility'.[10] Mill thinks his position unassailable, relying on practised self-consciousness and self-observation, assisted by observation of others.[11] He concedes, however, that in common language *virtue* is labelled as an end of conduct and that the utilitarian must recognize as a psychological fact the possibility of its being, to the individual, a good in itself, without looking to any end beyond it. This is not a counter-example, Mill contends, because virtue is in fact a means to happiness and could only be desired at all in the first place because it is so. Only then can it come to be desired for its own sake, its original end forgotten, though this association explains the possibility of its being an end.

This is of course a real counter-example. It does not matter how people come to value virtue as an end, only that in so doing they escape the shackles of hedonism. And this is reinforced by Mill's admission that virtue only *tends* to make us happy:[12] it does not always do so. This simply undermines Mill's case for happiness being the sole good.

Mill, however, has another argument to deal with what seem to be ends distinct from happiness. It is difficult to see such things as virtue as *means* to happiness, he argues, because they are in fact *part* of it. All the other ends of action are pursued because they come to be seen as parts or ingredients of the happy life. There is no real independence for such ends. It is worth noting that in reaching this conclusion Mill equivocates on the meaning of 'happiness'. Originally and ultimately Mill insists that happiness means pleasure, a psychological state. In the interim, in order to assimilate non-hedonistic ends to the end of happiness, he makes happiness a much fuller notion: it is something with ingredients made up of worthwhile activities and pursuits. Strictly speaking, however, these things can only have value as means to the generation of pleasure. And when we see this we see that the assimilation Mill requires is not possible. For how can these other ends be *part* of pleasure? How can the exercise of virtue be part of pleasure when that pleasure, as utilitarians insist, is a product of the activity. At best, then, these other ends have to be seen as means to pleasure. But Mill has already conceded that they are often desired 'without looking to any end beyond [them]'.[13] Clearly then, Mill makes a worse job of his hedonism than Bentham, and this must infect his whole proof. He fails to show that pleasure in itself is the sole end of all conduct.

What, then, of the final step in his argument, the derivation of the utility principle itself: the thesis that the general happiness ought to be the end of moral conduct? The argument behind the derivation seems to be a combination of several moves, most of them already familiar. It is often remarked of Mill's proof that it commits a logical fallacy, arguing

from (1) Each person's happiness is a good to that person,

to   (2) The happiness of everyone is a good to each person.

This is a fallacy because it simply does not follow. It is possible to care about my own happiness and be indifferent or worse to the happiness of others. However, it seems to me doubtful that this is the form Mill's argument takes. Rather, I suggest, he is trying to derive both statements from the simple assertion which precedes them, 'happiness is good'. Mill thinks he has shown from his previous psychological arguments that happiness is a good *per se*, and if he had, it seems to me that both the above statements follow. This, of course, is simply a rephrasing of Bentham's arguments concerning the good of dissociated pleasure, relying on the same faulty descriptions of the ends of even hedonistic action.

Mill, then, is no advance on Bentham in so far as the grounds of utilitarianism are concerned. The next major utilitarian thinker to offer a case was Sidgwick.[14] Sidgwick saw two great errors in Mill. First, he detected the contradictory adherence to both egoistic psychological hedonism and universal ethical hedonism (Sidgwick's way of characterizing utilitarianism). Second, he perceived the impossibility of deriving the universal utilitarian ethics from the individual's concern for his own welfare. More important for us is Sidgwick's rejection of Mill's method. He argues that 'the principle that pleasure is the only reasonable ultimate end of human action . . . cannot be known by induction from experience'.[15] By now we must be convinced of this. The ends people in fact aim at are often non-hedonistic or non-utilitarian. And, of course, it is no good trying to derive the principle inductively from 'rational' or 'moral' behaviour, for we have no means of identifying such behaviour in the requisite manner independently of the principle of utility itself, and to employ that would be circular. Further, if we try to derive the principle inductively from generally held moral beliefs we are likely to come across several which are decidedly anti-utilitarian. For example, many people think that criminals deserve to be punished and hence ought to be even if it does no good (as a deterrent, for instance). Even if we find that the great majority of moral beliefs, or the ones most dear to us, support the principle of utility's claim to be the supreme principle of morality, we still require a reason to acccept this as an adequate ground of a moral theory. (See Chapter 3 for a discussion of Rawls's use of this idea.)

Sidgwick instead relies on the device of intuition. It seemed to him intuitively certain that we ought to attempt to promote the maximum net balance of good that we can. For him, of those things in virtue of which we think of something as good, only experiences can really be so – and they are good or bad only in so far as they can be felt to be pleasant or painful. Thus pleasure is the only reasonable end of action, only pleasure has intrinsic goodness, and what ultimately underpins this is the intuition, delivered by introspection, that pleasure is a feeling which, when experienced by intelligent beings, is at least implicitly apprehended as desirable, or – in cases of comparison – preferable.[16] Sidgwick argues that all other apparently valuable ends lack this intuitive base and we are bound to dismiss them in favour of ethical hedonism.

Sidgwick, however, does not make the mistake of Bentham and Mill in thinking that he has found a universal end for rational action which transcends the interests of the agent concerned. He admits that egoism (the theory that the agent ought to pursue his own interests) is just as rational as utilitarianism (the theory that the agent ought to pursue everyone's interests). In the end we are left with a dualism of practical reason, an unsatisfactory result which Sidgwick tries to mitigate by arguing that enlightened egoism is almost equivalent in practice to utilitarianism. That this is an implausible suggestion is something of an understatement.

The strength of Sidgwick's argument is the way he defines the limits of the Benthamite grounds for utilitarianism. In identifying pleasure as the end of actions which may be self-interested or benevolent (and both may be rational) he exhausts the Benthamite position of utilitarian grounds. But he does not end up with pure utilitarianism. The weakness of his position is his reliance on intuition as a source of knowledge. To those of us who do not have this intuition or have others he can have little to say.

More recently attempts have been made to reach utilitarianism by imposing independently established *ethical* constraints on the pursuit of interests. Amongst such attempts are those of Peter Singer. He puts his case as follows:

> **Suppose I then begin to think ethically, to the extent of simply recognizing that my own interests cannot count for more, simply because they are my own, than the interests of others. In place of my own interests, I now have to take account of the interests of all those affected by my decision. This requires me to weigh up all these interests and adopt the course of action most likely to maximize the interests of those affected. Thus I choose the course of action which has the best consequences, on balance, for all affected. This is a form of utilitarianism.**[17]

Singer is trying to argue for the universal variety of ethical hedonism (though he replaces pleasure with the wider notion of 'interests') by dispensing with the egoistic strain on the grounds that universality (meaning impartiality) is an essential feature of ethical reasoning. He is correct in pointing out that universality is a pervasive feature of attempts to analyse moral thought. He has the support, for instance, of R. M. Hare,[18] who argues that the demand to universalize our judgements is ingrained in the language of morality, or, as he puts it, is part of the logic of moral concepts.

We may feel inclined to accept this characterization of the

ethical. But the argument for utilitarianism based on this is far more limited than those previously encountered. At best this argument will show that utilitarianism is the only ethical theory we can accept. It does not show, as Singer admits, that ethical conduct itself is rational or well-grounded – and this was something the original project certainly attempted.

The argument, to that extent, can only preach to the converted. Let us assume that we are, or want to be, moral. Must we then be utilitarians? The argument from universality above omits the crucial utilitarian premiss. We can agree with Singer that universality entails that interests may not be given preference *simply* in virtue of whose interests they are, but there are many other reasons we may have for ranking interests so that we are not indifferent as to whose they are. A particular individual may be more deserving, for example. The crucial missing premiss is that in addition to accepting that all interests are to count we must accept that interests as such are all that count in the final analysis.

It seems to me that the claim that only interests as such ultimately matter is a very strong claim as much in need of support as any other substantive moral claim. In particular here we should note that once we accept the legitimacy of bringing moral considerations into the argument (considerations such as universality) we have the problem of how to deal with those who may wish to bring in other moral considerations (such as moral desert, justice, human rights and so on). For all of these affect the way we would deal with interests (and, in effect, block the move to the maximizing policy).

Recognizing this, Singer contends that given the simplicity of his argument 'the onus of proof [is] on those who seek to go beyond utilitarianism',[19] meaning those who would attempt to derive further constraints on the way we are to pursue the good. Singer's view is that the 'utilitarian position is a minimal one', a first step we must take if we are to think morally, but which we may exceed only with very good reason.

To suppose utilitarianism a minimal position, it should be observed, is simply a function of holding a particular initial position – and Singer's initial position (that of trying to move from the egoist position to the moral) is in fact the one from which utilitarianism would seem a first step, a minimal move. But there is a serious question as to why, in constructing a moral theory, we should give egoism a privileged position. Certainly the egoist will be the major target for moral argument, but it is not clear why he should be granted such theoretical centrality. It is not clear why the position of the egoist should lend support to utilitarianism's claim to minimalism.

In any case, as I hope to demonstrate, it is not such a simple matter to move from a concern for welfare as basic to the claim that only interests count and then to the injunction to maximize the interests of those affected (where this means, I take it, maximizing the *meeting* of those interests). In order to show this I propose to examine a most perceptive analysis of the grounds and structure of utilitarianism proposed recently by Thomas Scanlon.[20]

Scanlon locates the appeal of utilitarianism in 'the thesis that the only fundamental moral facts are facts about individual well-being'.[21] Not only are such facts clearly central to moral deliberation and motivation, they seem to exhaust the possibilities of independent ultimate concerns. In the final analysis, something matters morally only if it matters for someone's well-being. What else, after all, could matter? The alternative is to adopt some kind of deontological ethics, an ethics which treats something else as an ultimate concern: something like the rightness of actions (breaking a promise or lying is wrong no matter what the consequences) or human rights (people have rights which must be observed no matter what the consequences). The trouble is that when we try to indicate why these things matter we seem forced to refer to their tendency to promote well-being in some way. In short, while the deontological position has great intuitive appeal, it seems to fall apart under rational scrutiny, and its concerns have to be given a derivative status (at best).

Scanlon calls this thesis 'philosophical utilitarianism' but we should notice that it is not (or not yet) distinctively utilitarian. It has not yet been asserted that well-being is to be understood as happiness (construed as a sum of pleasures). It would therefore be better to call this consequentialism at this stage. Scanlon, however, thinks that once *philosophical* utilitarianism has been accepted then some form of *normative* utilitarianism seems to be forced on us as the correct first order theory. His argument takes this form:[22]

1. All that counts morally is the well-being of individuals (in the final analysis).

2. No one individual counts for more than any other.

3. All that matters in the case of each individual is the degree to which his or her well-being is affected.

4. The basis of moral appraisal is the goal of maximizing the sum of individual well-being.

For the most part this argument is familiar. In (1) we have the assertion of the nature of the sole good. In (2) we have the move to dissociate this good from particular persons. And in (4) we have the familiar injunction to maximize the good (though this is not yet specified in the utilitarian way). Notice, however, that Scanlon has felt the need to add an additional premiss in (3). In seeing why this premiss is required we shall also see why the move from (1) to something distinctly utilitarian is problematic. However, Scanlon does not explain why (3) is included. What reasons are there?

To say that something counts is not to say *how* it counts. The second premiss is an attempt to rule out some forms of counting (those that would count only the well-being of good or deserving people, for example), and traditionally this has been thought adequate to produce the conclusion (4). However, there are other ways of counting which do not fit in with the utilitarian approach and which do not offend against (2). Consider the difference it would make if well-being were something you could either have or not have, there being no half-way house.* In that case the injunction in (4) might be to maximize the number of people who possess well-being. Next, consider that well-being is something we can have quantities of up until the point where we simply are well (we are leading a happy life). The fact that well-being is all that matters does not indicate in situations of scarcity whether it is more important to maximize the number who have well-being or to maximize aspects of well-being generally. In

---

* Consider in this context Plato's idea of knowledge of the form of the good, Christian ideas of being saved and the idea in other religions of becoming enlightened.

order to know that we have to know whether well-being is something we can attain and whether its attainment is of more importance than the previous approaches to it. For example, for some purposes becoming twenty-one is an important event. More important than becoming nineteen or twenty, though these are necessary steps on the way. If age were something we could distribute and becoming twenty-one were the ultimate end, it would be no good distributing years randomly since this would leave many younger than twenty-one and fewer twenty-one than is possible. Similarly in order to know how to deal with well-being we have to know what it is and how it matters – not just that it does.

In effect premiss (3) supplies the missing information. For it asserts that well-being is to count in the distinctive utilitarian manner. Well-being is something we can have as a matter of degree and all that matters is the degree to which we have it. There is, then, no equivalent of being aged twenty-one. And it is this information that is a necessary condition of the conclusion being reached.

Where, though, does premiss (3) come from? Not, it is clear, from philosophical utilitarianism. For that did not specify the nature of well-being in the required detail. The only source for this premiss, required in the derivation of normative utilitarianism, seems to be in a presumption that well-being is as the utilitarian requires – that it can be measured on a scale that admits no qualitative leaps (as, for example, the cooling of water results not just in cooler water but, ultimately, in ice). This, however, leaves the utilitarian again bereft of support, for there are, or could be, conceptions of well-being that render resort to the maximizing injunction inappropriate.

It needs stressing that this block of the route to a maximizing policy does not rest on some independent moral principle, as those who favour deontology would propose, but rather on the nature of well-being itself – in the possibility that it is not as the utilitarian requires it to be. I shall have more to say on this in the next section.

In the course of this section we have seen various weaknesses in the utilitarian project. Its attempt to demonstrate that pleasure is the sole good was seen to fail. Neither the methods of induction

47

or intuition are adequate. Further, because pleasure is not the sole human good, it is doubtful that it can simply be replaced by some other (fuller) conception in the utilitarian schema. For the demand to maximize requires that the good should be as the utilitarian imagines – composed of discrete entities, each of which is comparable and additive. We shall see this problem further highlighted when we turn to the question of what values the utilitarian espouses.

UTILITARIANISM AND POLITICAL VALUES

It is clear that utilitarian calculation about political affairs will be extremely complex. If we are to organize society along utilitarian lines we must have a wealth of information about what pleases people, from the food they eat to the social institutions they live with. Indeed these calculations are so complex that it has seemed to some that utilitarianism recommends nothing in particular except interminable debate about the expected pay-offs from the various possible structures we could create. And it must be conceded that *both* laissez-faire capitalism and state-controlled socialism can be given seemingly plausible utilitarian justifications. However, to many utilitarians such a confusion of output is obviated by a perceived bias in the very nature of the doctrine towards *equality*. This natural tendency of the utilitarian doctrine is perceived with the help of some simplifying assumptions.

First, the utilitarian reaches a presumption in favour of equality of resources (goods, income, money, etc.) on the basis of their diminishing marginal utility – a rich man would get less satisfaction from an additional allocation than would a poor man. Further, inequalities may in themselves produce disutility (by producing resentment and envy, and instilling desires and aspirations impossible to satisfy). The supposed requirements of utilitarianism to allocate resources unequally because more should be given to those who will get the most out of it (the more efficient converters of resources into utility) is denied, on the grounds that it is practically impossible to identify these people (on the whole – the class of the disabled may be an exception here) and the demand for equality of resources may then modulate into one for equality of welfare itself, on the same ground – that in equalizing we are maximizing.

This derivation of egalitarianism may be challenged, however. It is often argued that we can increase the production of resources and thus increase utility itself by offering incentives for effort, enterprise and so on. The utilitarian egalitarian may have to hold, with Marx, that the need for such incentives can be removed by altering the human personality (for instance, by getting rid of capitalism).

Another problem is that some people get pleasure at the cost of the suffering of others. If this takes a direct form (as in, for example, the rapist, the racist or the sexist) then the utilitarian will have to include the utility functions of such undesirables in his calculations. And if utilitarianism has to attend to desires that involve some people being treated unequally then it cannot be egalitarian. For example, if one half of the population, say men, desired the other half to be subservient, yet the other half only desired equality, then in the trade-off the resolution will occur somewhere between the two – but not at equality. However, the utilitarian egalitarian may be able to exclude such other-regarding desires on familiar grounds. For it does seem likely that more utility will result from ignoring them – or indeed in actively trying to change people so that they do not gain utility from such discordant sources.

There is, then, good, if not conclusive, reason to see utilitarianism as egalitarian, to see the demand to maximize welfare issuing in social structures which tend on the whole to equalize welfare. I say 'on the whole' because of course there have to be exceptions. It would, to say the least, be a novel approach to the problems of crime to attempt to make the criminal as happy as everyone else. Utilitarians generally consider that they have adequate grounds for an institution of punishment – usually in terms of protection and deterrence.

Here, however, we encounter a sample of what is thought to be the central weakness of utilitarianism: its inability to issue in *fair* social practices and institutions. For if it is justifiable on utilitarian grounds to punish offenders in order to deter, then it seems that it will also be justifiable to punish innocent people in certain situations for the same end. It is not that the utilitarian is indifferent as to whom he would like punished. The innocent tend to be more upset by being punished than do the guilty. However, if the guilty party cannot be found and someone else can be easily 'framed' then perhaps it would be a good idea to do so. This would deter just as well and foster confidence in the police force's abilities to catch criminals – though, of course, the fact that the person is innocent and that such a practice goes on would have to be kept secret (for obvious reasons).

This is but one example of what is commonly considered utilitarianism's inadequacy. Not only does it ignore what we take to be important and directly salient features of a case (such as guilt), it seems unable to provide that its prescriptions should be extensionally equivalent (that is, do the same things albeit for different reasons). Utilitarianism seems destructive of something we hold most dear, justice or fairness.

Again, however, the utilitarian has a response. In the first place we cannot assume that it is never justified to sacrifice an innocent person to prevent a great harm or attain a great good. Many people have done just this to appease their God, for example. And if their beliefs were true would they not be justified in doing so? Perhaps, it may be said, if the victim were selected in a fair way. Second, it is far from clear that a generalized practice of punishing the innocent could be justified on utilitarian grounds. Such a practice would have to be kept secret, something very difficult in an open society. It would have to be entrusted to public officials and it is doubtful that people who could do this routinely are the sort of people best suited to public life. In any case, no such practice would be isolated; and its mentality would infect all areas of public life. Can we seriously suggest that those countries in the world which indulge in such practices have the utilitarian's support? In designing social structures we have to be aware of human weakness, stupidity and malevolence. We must provide against abuse. It is not, then, unlikely that the social structures with the greatest utility will be those which observe justice, at least in some plausible sense of that term. And when justice is to be sacrificed for some great good (to save humanity, perhaps) the utilitarian at least has a case to offer. He may well be correct in rejecting the idea of *fiat iustitia, pereat mundus*.

Perhaps, then, utilitarianism is a coherent theory, and

perhaps also it will issue some determinate social prescription. The final question we must ask is whether this view of the good society is one we can endorse. The way in which I have pursued this question was via a consideration of the way the principle of utility is derived, for that derivation reveals what I think is a real weakness in the theory. It begins by identifying the sole, ultimate value as happiness, a sum of pleasure-states. This is its objective theory of the human good. In addition, and for obvious reasons, the utilitarian recommends a maximizing policy. The theory at least is tight and clear. Given its nature, however, attention is immediately drawn to the utilitarian theory of the good.

We can all agree, in Aristotelian fashion, that the good life comprises happiness (well-being or even welfare) but we are only agreeing on a name. If we understand the utilitarian as attempting to formulate the structure of a society which caters maximally for the good life in its citizenry (whether by direction, encouragement or merely negatively, by creating the conditions of its possibility through choice, for example) we have to ask whether the human good really is as the utilitarian conceives it. In the earlier discussion of the grounds of utilitarianism it was argued that the demand to maximize requires more than a theory of the good and the claim that only this ultimately matters. It requires that the good be the kind of thing that can be maximized – a measurable, scalar entity. It is only because utility is such an entity that the maximization demand is rational.

However, if the human good cannot be conceived in this manner, if, for example, we have to recognize a diversity of irreducible elements in the good life, the utilitarian approach will be misconceived. Perhaps an analogy will make this clearer. If we say that the good diet largely comprises fruit and vegetables, it is sensible to advise people to maximize the amount of fruit and vegetables they consume (as a proportion of all consumption). But if we say, more correctly, that the good diet is made up of a certain quantity of food, balanced with respect to protein, carbohydrates, fats, minerals and vitamins, what then are we to maximize? Certainly we can maximize the number of elements in the diet which go to make up the good diet. But this is not to maximize any particular element in the diet, still less the good diet itself. It is better described as a closer approximation to the good diet.

If the human good is like this then it may be better to say that the good life is something we can be closer to or further from rather than something we can have more and more of. Still, it may be argued that the utilitarian mentality simply re-emerges in a demand to maximize the number of people who experience the good life. But while this is a concern of obvious attraction it is not the only option. In a situation of scarcity it is not clear whether it is better to maximize the numbers of those living the good life (at the expense of others) or to try to bring everyone as close to the good life as possible. We cannot derive an answer to this as the utilitarian suggests, for we need to know the relative importance of living the good life and of living the various approximations to it.

It is the supposed nature of utility itself which allows the utilitarian to ignore these problems. However, the question we must ask is whether this reduced conception of the value constitutes a minimal demand, as Singer thinks, or whether it is altogether too great a demand to place on any plausible theory of the good.

As noted earlier, there can be lesser demands than the full utilitarian one. We could, for example, endorse 'negative' utilitarianism which enjoins the minimization of suffering rather than the maximization of benefit. However, not only does this suggestion require the same of the good as full utilitarianism (in the way of homogeneity and measurability), it then makes an irrational concession in the pursuit of the good. For if the good is as the utilitarian conceives it then maximization is the only rational demand.

The main problem facing utilitarianism here is that it does not seem to take seriously the ideal of a person framing a plan of life, something which gives meaning to his life as a whole. The utilitarian sees this as a derivative concern, preferring that life (or even that part of a life) which has the greatest net utility. But this seems to invert the proper order of priority, which sees the value of pleasure deriving from its contribution to the good life and not vice versa. For example, it does seem incongruous that the evil man's pleasure in his evil acts is valuable in itself.

More generally, utilitarianism defines the ultimate value in what we might call a reductive way. While it is implausible to deny that pleasure is a good thing, indeed that a life without pleasure could hardly be considered a good life, it is simply not possible to construct a recognizable candidate for the good life from the pursuit of pleasure *simpliciter*.

Utilitarianism locates the ultimate object of concern in a time slice of an individual's psychological state (the experience of pleasure). The example of a pleasure machine which stimulates our pleasure centres to which we could permanently attach ourselves shows that pleasure is not a distinctively human good. Would it make sense to say that all of our distinctively human capacities – our ability to reason, pursue knowledge, form social relationships and so on – are in themselves irrelevant to our good?

Consider someone who can choose whether or not to take heroin. If he does, he reasons he will have a (shortish) life of relative bliss and (he hopes) a painless death from a final overdose – we need not worry, here, whether this is an adequate picture of a possibility. For the utilitarian this is a candidate for the good life (at least for some). It may be rational, in his view, to shorten one's life if in so doing one experiences a greater amount of pleasure. Following Aristotle, however, we would see the good life as a complete life, exhausting our three score and ten; a life made up of 'healthy' activities in which pleasure plays (only) a part. Utilitarianism only contingently (if at all) endorses a recognizably good life and for a political philosophy which places goodness in the foundational role this is a source of structural failure.

We have reason, then, to doubt the utilitarian theory of the good. And, as we have seen, if this theory is replaced by a fuller one (one going beyond pleasure) we have reason to doubt the applicability of a maximizing policy. It may be replied, however, that this is not really decisive. For if utilitarianism can generate political values of equality and liberty, then in the good society there will be provision for lives which are not simply hedonistic. The utilitarian may be able to say that within a framework of rough economic equality more pleasure is produced by letting people pursue the lives they themselves find valuable.

Perhaps there is some truth in this. There is a case for saying that those societies which we call liberal democracies have higher levels of pleasure than most others. But the point is that the utilitarian cannot claim that this justifies these political values or the societies which observe them. Liberty and equality may be important political values but not for the reasons utilitarians say.

For those who hold such values the response to the utilitarian should be this: You may have reached correct conclusions, but your premises are false and your argument unsound. What possible support can your theory give to these ideals? This, curiously enough, has been the response of many contemporary liberal democrats to utilitarianism. They fear that utilitarianism justifies something else entirely, something less than acceptable as a candidate for the good society. It is to the most prominent of such responses that I now turn.

3.

JOHN RAWLS
AND THE CONTRACTARIAN
CONCEPTION OF JUSTICE

The overall aim of Rawls's project is to develop a systematic alternative to utilitarianism, or more generally any teleological theory. The major defect of such theories, according to Rawls, is that by subordinating the notion of right to that of the good (and for utilitarians 'right' means 'the cause of a good result') an adequate theory of justice becomes impossible.

> **Each person possesses an inviolability founded on justice that even the welfare of society as a whole cannot override.**[1]

Teleological theories, Rawls argues, fail to respect this inviolability since they will treat it as a dispensable means to the overall end. Rawls therefore prefers an independent source for his theory of justice. This is what he means when he talks of 'the priority of the right over the good'. What is right (justice) is to be established independently from what is good, or what makes for the most good.

Rawls thus works with two theories, one of right or justice and one of the good. Both are required because 'all ethical doctrines worth our attention take consequences into account in judging rightness. One which did not would simply be irrational, crazy.'[2] The novelty of Rawls's approach, then, is his attempt to develop a deontological theory which none the less admits the importance of consequences. In essence it is a compromise theory with all of the strengths and weaknesses that label usually implies.

To achieve his compromise Rawls deploys a novel theory of the good – of what should be the proper object of distributive concern. The good is not, as in teleological theory, ultimate or intrinsic. It is instead a set of goods deemed to be universally useful – things that are useful no matter what ends a person may pursue. These are called 'social primary goods', and comprise liberties, opportunities, income and wealth and the bases of self-respect. They are conceived as those universally desirable goods which society's social structures directly control.

The allocation of these goods is the concern of justice. In order that the allocation be just, Rawls suggests that we should attend to the basic structures of society, that is, the major social institutions. These play the major role in allocating social primary goods and are therefore the primary subject of justice.

But what does justice consist in? It is not, for Rawls, to be equated with that system which maximizes the good (say, maximizes the enjoyment of social primary goods). It is an independent theory. Since the theory of the good cannot by itself be the source of principles of right, justice must have some other source. What Rawls proposes is a notion of 'fairness', and this is intended to represent a set of independent ethical constraints. There are to be constraints of fairness on what people may do to one another even (or especially) in pursuit of the good. This, as Rawls sees it, will remedy the major failing of utilitarianism.

However, we now have the problem of defining fairness.

There is substantial disagreement over the nature of fairness (and hence justice). There are three standard views on this: fairness demands that we distribute goods according to merit (or desert), needs, or rights. Rawls has a more complicated view of a proper distribution and, again, a novel view of how this conception of fairness is to be justified. His basic idea is inspired by traditional social-contract theory. We are to imagine a group of people coming together in order to formulate principles which will govern the allocation of social primary goods via society's basic structures. It is Rawls's contention that in virtue of the concerns which he ascribes to these people (they are rationally self-interested and non-envious), the knowledge which they possess (they know general facts about the human sciences but are ignorant of certain facts about themselves – they do not know who they will be in actual life), and the options presented to them, they will choose Rawls's principles and that the principles will thereby be justified.

In the next section we shall examine Rawls's case for his conception of 'justice as fairness'. Here I shall explain Rawls's principles and the kind of society which Rawls thinks they justify.

Initially, Rawls argues that his contractors will choose a principle of presumptive equality:

All social primary goods are to be distributed equally unless an unequal distribution is to the advantage of everyone.[3]

This can be better understood, perhaps, if we concentrate on the fate of that group which would be worst off in an unequal distribution. That group, Rawls insists, must be better off than in an equal distribution if any inequalities are to be justified.

This criterion gives way to a more complex version, however, in a situation of relative affluence (such as the modern developed world). This is because the various social primary goods take on different degrees of importance – or so Rawls has it. These goods divide into three classes which are, in order of importance, the basic liberties (a range of economic, personal, intellectual and political freedoms), opportunities to achieve desired positions, and income and wealth. Accordingly, the original principle becomes three, and again these are ranked in the following order of importance:

1. The principle of greatest equal liberty;
2. The principle of fair equality of opportunity;
3. The principle of difference.

What these principles enjoin is given by replacing 'the relevant class of social primary goods' for 'all social primary goods' in the formulation given above. The important point here is the ranking of principles. Rawls assigns them a 'lexical order', which is the order given above, meaning that a prior principle is to be fully complied with before later ones are considered.

What we have, then, is priority (absolute priority) ascribed to liberty over equality of opportunity and these in turn over welfare. The priority, of course, is not of these goods themselves but of everyone's enjoyment of them. In this way Rawls hopes to have codified the value system of what we may call 'social democracy' or 'welfare liberalism'.

In reality Rawls wants to offer a justification of societies not unlike the modern Western democracies. There will be a 'free-enterprise' economy with private ownership of capital and natural resources. This will be regulated by the state, using mostly macro-economic techniques, in order to promote reasonably full employment and low inflation. For those who are unable to find work or are otherwise unable to support themselves, social security (financed by taxation) will ensure a decent income. In short Rawls is reasonably confident that our structural arrangements are just. We must now attempt to discover whether or not that confidence is well placed.

THE ORIGINAL POSITION

Rawls presents his principles of justice as the choice of people in the original position. Why do this? What kind of support is this meant to lend the principles?

The answer to this is that the original position is meant to embody 'contractarianism', a theory which has its origins in traditional social-contract theory 'as found, say, in Locke, Rousseau and Kant'.[4] Thus the cogency of the theory requires three things. First, that the people in the original position choose the principles. Second, that this choice reflects a contract. Third, that this way of choosing somehow renders the principles just.

The intuitive case for Rawls's thought experiment is obvious enough. The original position captures something of what we think of as *procedural* fairness. To give a similar instance, imagine you are to cut a cake into shares. Some would say that a fair procedure here is that you get last choice of a piece of it. Similarly, in designing the original position, Rawls is trying to ensure that no one can take unfair advantage of the fact that they are framing the rules. The key idea here is that people in the original position are behind a 'veil of ignorance' so that they do not know, as it were, which piece of cake they will get. The conditions on the original position are intended to produce just this kind of fair result.

However, let us begin by examining the first of the three requirements given above. Do the people in the original position choose the principles Rawls says they do?

There are two main doubts here. The first is Rawls's insistence that it is rational for his contractors to employ a *maximin* strategy in the choice of principles. The second concerns the ranking of social primary goods so as to give priority to liberty.

The maximin strategy is presented by Rawls as the rational outlook of people in the original position. Informed rationality, as Rawls conceives it, enjoins the maximization of one's share of social primary goods. In the original position, however, a person cannot be this directly concerned with his own interests, but only with his interests *whatever they turn out to be*. And because not everyone's interests can be maximized at once (there being conflicting interests and scarce resources) a more complex form of rational choice is required. The first approximation to consider is to prefer an equal distribution of social primary goods. This ensures that no one will end up with an 'unduly' small share, that no one will fare badly in a relative way. But this is irrational if there is an allocation which produces more goods in total and which will render no one worse off compared to an equal distribution. Such a situation may be possible if the provision of incentives encourages some to produce more than otherwise and if the benefits from this greater product can be shared out to some extent. In this respect society may not be like a cake, for the social product may vary with social arrangements.

Rawls, however, claims that only those inequalities which

would make the worst-off better off (than in equality) would be acceptable to someone in the original position. Any inequality must be to everyone's advantage. In this, Rawls would seem to be overly biased in favour of equality. Why should a non-envious person begrudge someone else their good fortune if this does not make him actually worse off? However, the irrationality of this bias is less clear than may be supposed from what Rawls says. For in order that a worse-off group remain as well off after the introduction of an inequality it must be made better off. And this for two reasons.

First, the worse-off have to be compensated for the introduction of the inequality because that inequality will undermine at least one important social primary good – self-respect. This is not because of envy. It is simply because those that do less well will feel inferior.

Second, when someone becomes better off others are necessarily made worse off, since their bargaining power in the market for scarce goods is reduced. The price of scarce resources will rise as some become capable of more effective demand (that is, can pay more).

Thus it would seem wise of people in the original position to be suspicious of inequalities which do not adequately compensate those left behind. But while this kind of reasoning may help resolve the apparent irrationality in Rawls's strategy, it still leaves open the question of why there is such concern with equality in the first place. Rawls's case rests on his claim that people in the original position will be concerned to maximize their probable share of social primary goods in a very cautious way. This is the 'maximin' strategy – it is thought rational to ensure that the worst that can befall one is as good as possible.

The selection of this strategy is highly controversial. In effect it places the whole burden of justification on the notion of rationality built into the original position – or more accurately on the personalities of the people therein. Let us look briefly at each of the elements of maximin: caution and greed.

Rawls argues that people in the original position will value primary goods in such a way that they will choose principles which make their worst prospects best; they choose the safest option. Indeed they proceed as though their own worst enemy will assign them their place in the scheme of things. For Rawls this is what elevates his own theory above utilitarianism. The great failing of that theory is that it may buy higher aggregate utility by imposing severe hardship (even slavery) on some. A person in the original position would not risk being one of these, so will reject the principle of utility in favour of maximin.

The caution Rawls builds into the personality of his contractors is unconvincing, however. On the straightforward economic view of rationality which Rawls endorses, people will simply calculate probable benefits and burdens and seek to maximize their probable share of utility. There is nothing irrational, at least as economic rationality sees it, in risking life and limb for the prospect of great riches (if the odds are reasonable).

A fuller conception of rationality and personality is thus required, and Rawls tries to flesh out the bare economic model of man he begins with. First, he observes that people in the original position will be concerned that their whole lives are good (whatever view of the good life they will happen to endorse in real life). They will therefore refrain from any risky strategy since the stakes are so high. There are two things wrong with this, however. First, one cannot rule out knowledge of what people will think to be the good life and at the same time insist that they endorse the Aristotelian view that whatever else it will be a complete life. There are other conceptions of the good life, such as 'Live for today and let tomorrow look after itself', which undermine Rawls's case. Second, the fact that the stakes are high does not in itself alter the rationality of a risky strategy. Indeed, it could be argued that a gamble is only worthwhile when the stakes are high.

A second attempt by Rawls to justify the caution of his contractors consists in the value he attributes to self-respect. Any risky strategy may consign one to a life of misery or degradation, the life of a slave perhaps, so would not possibly be entertained. Again, however, this looks weak. Quite why self-respect should be given this weight in our deliberations is a mystery and in any case it is surely possible to miss out on life's luxuries without losing one's self-respect. Even slaves have been known to be proud.

A third consideration is this. People in the original position know that if they end up as slaves they will feel hard done by and be unable to accept their lot. Since the choice in the original position is an honest commitment, they cannot commit themselves to any strategy which they could not endorse in real life. But again this is unconvincing. Many people do make large bets and 'lose their shirts'. Not all of them find cause for complaint in this. After all, they were not cheated and nor would Rawls's contractors be.

None of these considerations is of much use in justifying a cautious strategy. Further, they are unavailable from Rawls's theoretical viewpoint. He repeats a well-known error, often associated with Kant's moral philosophy, of relying on a particular well-defined notion of the self when all his theory will allow is the rational self of economic theory.

People in the original position, therefore, have no reason to be as cautious as Rawls claims. This is more obvious still if they are offered some strategy less risky than utilitarianism threatens to be. For example, they might consider utilitarianism subject to some proviso – say, arrange society so as to maximize utility so long as no one is more than twice as well off as anyone else; or that inequalities are to be allowed so long as no one falls below the 'poverty line' (and this is the sort of thing which Rawls ends up with anyway).

The other aspect of the proposed rational strategy is the concern to maximize shares of social primary goods. Now this the economic theory of rationality seems to endorse. But we have to be convinced that this view of rationality is the correct one. Rationality, on this interpretation, is the efficient pursuit of one's ends, whatever those ends happen to be. And Rawls thinks that the concern to maximize one's share of primary goods is rational since these goods are universal means to any reasonable conception of the good life. But this is simply false. As we saw in our discussion of utilitarianism there are reasonable conceptions of the good life which do not entail the rationality of a maximizing approach. What has this to do, for example, with the search for 'enlightenment' or 'wisdom'? Would it not, indeed, sometimes hinder the pursuit of such ends to have to cope with a society intent on ensuring that one had the best possible share of social primary goods?

Finally, regarding the choice of principles, what are we to make of Rawls's claim that of the social primary goods *liberties* are to be given priority? It is important to be clear what this priority consists in before we assess the case for it. Rawls is not making the implausible claim that liberties are everywhere and always to be the most highly ranked of social primary goods. This priority only emerges in the context of a reasonably wealthy society and the point, I take it, is that such societies are able to guarantee everyone the means of subsistence. Liberty, then, does not have absolute priority – in fact, its priority is spurious since it depends on the fact that other, more basic, goods are already provided. In Chapter 6 I shall argue that this list of goods can be extended to include such things as pleasure, activities involving work and leisure, and certain characteristic human relationships (such as friendship). And instead of ascribing priority to liberty we shall see it as essentially enabling for the good life only if it contributes to the enjoyment of these goods.

Rawls, however, rejects the idea that a theory of the good may play this role. His idea is that people in the original position are to choose goods under the description of universal means, means which serve any end. The problem is that liberty does not seem to be such a means. All being free means is that social structures are not going to stand in the way of our 'doing our own thing' (provided that does not involve harming others). But other things can and do stand in our way – not least our own competence, weakness of will or cowardice. Curiously, Rawls accepts this, for he offers the traditional case for paternalism (limiting people's freedom for their own good).[5] But how can something be a social primary good, a universally effective or valuable means, yet not be? If Rawls's case for paternalism is good (and it seems sensible) how can it be rational for people in the original position to treat liberty as a social primary good, and worse, assign it priority amongst them?

It would seem doubtful, then, that the original position will deliver Rawls's principles. However, the question remains, even if hypothetically, what kind of support is the original position? What kind of argument is it? Could it be used, perhaps, to support something else?

As noted, Rawls presents the choice of principles as a kind

of social-contract theory. Whatever the merits of that particular approach, however, it does not seem that Rawls's theory is contractarian. Let us examine the main differences.

The original position, or 'pre-contract' situation, is purely hypothetical, so that any justification that might be gained from an actual agreement (as in, say, making a promise) is not to the point. Likewise, because every person in the original position is identical in every respect there is no reality even to a hypothetical *bargaining* situation. As Rawls says,

> It is clear that since the differences among the parties are unknown to them, and everyone is equally rational and similarly situated, each is convinced by the same arguments. Therefore, we can view the choice in the original position from the standpoint of one person selected at random.[6]

Rawls seems to think that this merely simplifies the bargaining problem, but in fact it means that there is no bargaining game at all – only a uniform-choice situation. In effect there is only one party involved. A proper game, and indeed a social contract, requires that the parties know their own conflicting interests and can calculate a proper strategy. In Rawls's game there is no real conflict because any set of interests could turn out to be those that a particular person in the original position will have. He is forced, in effect, to be concerned with everyone's interests.

Similarly, there is no reality to any non-contract situation. In a real contract situation people always have to consider the pay-offs involved in reaching no agreement. That this is irrelevant in Rawls's theory shows that the contractarian trappings are merely for show. What the original position turns out to be is a mere choosing situation – a person chooses rather than bargains or contracts. What kind of choice situation is this? No doubt, for Rawls, it is an ideal one, for he claims that it embodies the 'circumstances of justice'[7] and because of its fairness will in fact issue in principles of social justice. The essential question is what kind of support, if any, does the original position lend the principles (whatever they are) chosen therefrom?

To survive, then, the theory needs to be re-described and the comparison I wish to pursue is with ideal-observer theory. There are two main reasons for this. First, Rawls's theory is best seen as a modification of utilitarianism rather than a radical alternative to it. In particular, we must question whether Rawls has succeeded in rejecting teleology. For a non-teleological theory would surely dissociate itself from end-states in a more radical way than does Rawls's.

This structural similarity follows from the aggregative nature of the theory and from the motivations of the choosers, given the conditions of ignorance. It might be argued, however, that the original position can be structurally distinguished from utilitarianism since choices

> **made in deliberate abstraction from empirical information which actually exists are necessarily from a utilitarian point of view irrational, and to that extent the formal structure of the outlook, even allowing the admission of general empirical information, is counter-utilitarian.**[8]

But it is not clear why this imposes a structural divergence. In particular it is not obvious that the particular information omitted is relevant to utilitarian calculation. The veil of ignorance actually accords well with the utilitarian abstraction from individual identity and the condition that each is to count for one and only one. Indeed people in the original position actually engage in utility calculation. An actual contract is one way of introducing a structural distinction but, as I have argued, Rawls's theory is essentially non-contractarian.

The second feature that invites our comparison is the fact that Rawls's original position, like the viewpoint of the impartial spectator, has unrestricted scope: it is intended as a model of the moral point of view as such. It is this way of looking at the two theories which leads Rawls himself to invite the comparison,[9] and it is to a fuller investigation of this that I now turn.

The original position, I shall argue, may be interpreted as a heuristic device which expresses, or tries to, the constraints of moral reasonableness after the fashion of ideal-observer theory. Of course Rawls has a much more elaborate and well-defined conception of this viewpoint but I think a direct line can be traced to the theory of Rawls from the beginnings of the modern ideal-observer theory in the thought of Smith[10] and Hume.[11] The device of the ideal observer is an attempt to raise one's viewpoint above the merely prudential in order to judge human affairs morally in that it is intended to specify the proper limits of egoism and self-referential altruism (for example, in the parable of the good Samaritan) and the common good. The ideal observer is one who encompasses the viewpoint of justice and sees the totality of human life, treating the interests of each person on their merits. He is an impartially benevolent spectator and the imaginative exercise of 'becoming' him helps us to be impartial between persons, to exclude bias in the shape of personal preference.

Impartiality is understood to mean that a reaction or judgement is not influenced by the fact that some special individual or group is involved. Certainly Rawls holds that the original position is a device for excluding bias, for guaranteeing objectivity, enabling us to 'look at the social world from the required point of view'.[12] He clearly expresses an ideal-observer commitment in the final sentence of his book: 'Purity of heart, if one could attain it, would be to see clearly and to act with grace and self-command from this point of view.' Most explicitly the veil of ignorance is intended to '. . . nullify the effects of specific contingencies which put men at odds and tempt them to exploit social and natural circumstances to their own advantage'.[13]

We should note that this is not, of course, a meta-ethical view, a theory about the meaning of moral language. While Rawls has very little to say on this subject it is clear that he does not claim that in saying something is wrong, for example, we *mean* that someone in the original position would choose to legislate against it. And equally obviously we need not consider the implausible interpretation of ideal-observer theory to the same effect. Our attention must focus on the substantive results of these theories, for they are devices designed to explicate or re-describe our moral thought rather than attempts at lexicography.

We may begin with Rawls's own reason for distancing his theory from that of the ideal observer. This is that he discerns 'a natural derivation of the classical principle of utility'[14] from the latter. Satisfaction utilitarianism is indifferent to the separateness of those who have the satisfaction, and the ideal observer (which adopts 'for society as a whole the principle of rational choice for one man')[15] is seen as a model for this agglomeration.

In fact, as Rawls notes, there is much more to the link

between ideal-observer theory and satisfaction utilitarianism than this. Something like the device of Humean sympathy and the utilitarian reduction of individualism must be combined to complete the link. Thus there is no more reason to take the ideal-observer theory as a model for the agglomeration of impersonal satisfaction than the original position itself, since in both any such agglomeration is a function of the preferences ascribed to, on the one hand, an ideal observer and, on the other, to a person in the original position.

Another obvious objection is that Rawls's choosers are greatly ignorant, as opposed to an ideal observer who has all relevant knowledge. This same claim is made by Rawls, however, concerning his 'contractors', for they are thought to have all the knowledge relevant to the choice which they have to make. I take it then that the original position can be seen as a modification to traditional ideal-observer theory in an attempt to overcome its shortcomings – such as vagueness (just what would the observer say?). Thus self-interest and the veil of ignorance combine to form Rawls's way of forcing a determinate choice which is at the same time impartial. We may describe the people in the original position, on Rawls's behalf, as ideally ignorant. This modification is implicitly recognized by Rawls in his appeal to the deductive power of the original position.[16]

Assuming, then, that we have established something of a parallel here, what are we to make of the result? There are several powerful objections to ideal-observer theory, most obviously the relativist one that to imagine oneself as an impartial spectator is simply to abstract one's own moral code (or prejudice), giving it a universal status. Rawls's only response to this seems to be his doctrine of reflective equilibrium, something we shall examine later.

This commitment to ideal-observer theory actually goes some way to retaining the perspective of social-contract theory, which we have noted is itself absent in any real form. Social-contract theory was pre-eminently designed to ensure that in the framing of the basic rules of the game, the constitution, each party's interests were equally weighted; it strove for interpersonal impartiality. The conditions of the original position, and in particular the veil of ignorance, are similarly designed to guarantee that the principles chosen will be fair and unbiased as amongst persons. But the constraints of the original position follow social-contract theory and go beyond traditional ideal-observer theory in that they make certain that the principles chosen will not systematically favour any conception of the good life; no plan of life can be favoured simply because it more fully incorporates some aspect of human well-being, for the choice must be neutral on the question of the good life.

It turns out that the conditions of fairness and impartiality built into the original position are specifically liberal in a familiar sense of that term – Dworkin's.[17] Political liberalism (the attachment to some form of pluralist and limited democracy, of individual liberty and so on) may be supported by various philosophical theories, for example, by utilitarianism (like Mill), or by natural rights (as in the constitution of the USA). In theory, however, each of these philosophies could support something else; utilitarianism could support a meritocracy, natural rights a form of anarchy.

However, the original position is defined in such a way as to encapsulate what Dworkin calls the constitutive morality of political liberalism.[18] That morality is founded on the idea of neutrality; that the government ought to be neutral on the question of the good life; that the principles of justice ought to be so neutral. Further it seems to be a consequence of this approach, indeed it is implicit in the method of reflective equilibrium, that if the original position does not deliver a recognizable form of political liberalism then it must be revised. However, as we shall see, the original position does indeed incorporate such neutrality via the veil of ignorance and this takes its toll in terms of justification. There are other conceptions (morally fuller ones) of fairness and impartiality which need not produce principles of justice neutral amongst different plans of life and conceptions of the good. And so this aspect of Rawls's method is seen to beg the question, for the original position by itself cannot justify this approach.

This *philosophically* liberal aspect of Rawls's thought reveals itself in both the conception of human nature he builds into the original position and the role he assigns to primary goods in his thin theory of the good.

Human nature, as abstracted in the original position, has two main features. People therein are rational 'in the narrow sense, standard in economic theory, of taking the most effective means to a given end'[19] and mutually disinterested, 'conceived as not taking an interest in one another's interests'.[20] The reason for this is that we are 'to avoid introducing ... any controversial ethical elements'.[21] The features Rawls adopts are those that make up the abstract individual of liberal theory and classical political economy (how else, indeed, could the choice problem be decidable?). Yet this is simply to confuse a specific social character with human nature itself. Marx observed that Bentham went in search of human nature and found the English shopkeeper. Rawls, it seems, is as convinced as Hume was that human nature is much the same in all times and places, and concludes that liberalism is the universal morality. What is needed, and what is not given (for the original position could not do so), are arguments for philosophical liberalism, arguments in favour, say, of moral scepticism[22] and the ultimacy of individual choice in matters of morals. Rawls offers no such arguments, indeed would not do so, since he believes otherwise.

This ungrounded liberalism is also a consequence of the use of the partial conception of abstract man Rawls employs to ground his theory of the good. This can be explicated as follows. The original position presents Rawls with a problem. Individuals are to choose principles of political right but they cannot choose them under that description since they have no morality. Their choice is a function of their (redefined) self-interest – that is, they have to choose perceived goods or ends. But because Rawls eschews teleology in that in 'justice as fairness the concept of right is prior to that of the good',[23] the theory of the good to which a theory of justice refers must be stripped down to its bare essentials. This is intended to remove the ethical import of the choice in that the thin theory of the good sees the object of choice as primary goods – those goods which are universal means. 'Rational individualists, whatever else they want, desire certain other things as prerequisites for carrying out their plans of life.'[24] Thus 'it is rational to want these goods whatever else is wanted, since they are in general necessary for the framing and the execution of a rational plan of life'.[25] This, it is thought, will impose the priority of right over any definitive conception of the good life.

People in the original position want primary goods, it seems, because these will be useful no matter what else they may want. Rawls thinks his primary goods are neutral amongst plans of life but plainly this is not so. Some plans of life actually require the absence of primary goods, for example, being a Christian (on some interpretations) or an ascetic. If it be replied that they have the option to give up their wealth we need only imagine an ascetic suffering from weakness of the will. He does not want a social system which is constantly attempting to undermine his self-denial by offering to maximize his worst-off position. If it be further argued that this is not an example of a rational life-plan then we must ask from what standpoint this judgement is made. Is it not from a morally loaded one such as that of the materialistic liberal? Similarly, if it be argued that people in the original position would not choose such strange lifestyles since the view of the good involved is irrelevant, then the argument is surely lost. For these lifestyles do exist and are valued by some (materially sane) people. People in the original position must therefore accept the possibility of their being amongst that number and calculate accordingly. If they are nevertheless forced to dismiss these ways of life (and the limitation to choose so as to optimize primary goods-holding in some way seems to do this) then the original position fails in its own terms; it is not liberal, for it does indeed contain some notion (an ethical notion) of preferred lifestyles.

Similarly, the contention that Rawls is smuggling liberalism into his method is strengthened by his own admission that he does not hold that 'criteria of excellence lack a rational basis . . .'[26] For if such criteria do have a rational basis then how can we fail to use them in the formulation of judgements of morals. His reason for rejecting fuller conceptions of the good than his own version (even a demonstrably true one) is that accepting one such into his theory would not be compatible with his 'rejection of the principle of perfection and the acceptance of democracy in the assessment of one another's excellences'.[27] These, it seems, 'have no special merit from the standpoint of justice'.[28]

But surely this is a strange way of dismissing human good,

excellence and virtue. If the original position is meant to incorporate the moral point of view, how can it ignore these moral notions while accepting them as rationally based? Clearly a liberal theory might want to do so, but the problem is over the grounds of so doing. Here, it seems, Rawls joins the ranks of those who worship freedom as an end in itself, favouring the right to choose over any objective standards morality may try to impose. Such a view of the value of freedom is untenable but in any case it sits ill at ease in the company of Rawls's social democracy, which seeks to curtail such freedom in favour of welfare. Further, it is not the freedom of real people which is valued (as in the theory of Nozick, for example) but the freedom of an abstraction whose choice has value mainly in the terms of its outcome, an outcome which is a 'forced' choice.

We can see, then, that the original position, the characteristics of the people therein and the objects of choice specified combine to make the principles chosen liberal principles. The device which makes this most explicit is the veil of ignorance which forces people to be neutral on the question of the good life.

It turns out that the object of Rawls's *A Theory of Justice* was to explicate proper social relations in terms of the right of everyone to an equal concern and respect as moral beings in the design of common institutions.[29] But because of the veil of ignorance, the concern and respect involved are those a rational egoist has for himself, but generalized, that is, we are forced to consider the plans and projects of others as worthy as our own, or indeed as worthy as any objective ideals which may exist. Now while it may be thought that an egoist behind the veil of ignorance has some claim to epitomize the moral point of view in that he regards everyone 'out there' as potentially himself (that is, he cares, in effect, for everyone else in the same way and as much as for himself), it is surely going too far to insist that plans of life (even within the limits imposed by the harm principle, for example) are untouched by moral insight. And Rawls embodies liberalism in his method in just this assertion.

If we characterize modern liberalism by the thesis that the good life for man cannot be, or ought not to be, decided from the public standpoint (that is, individuals must be free to frame and pursue their own conception of the good subject to the limits of harmony) then it can be seen that Rawls's methodological devices actually presuppose and, not surprisingly, deliver this. It is not, then, even a relevant question whether there is a good life for man (as Aristotle thought). Rather Rawls's method assumes there is not, that men have to create their own vision of a good life as they see fit, and do so as individuals – there being no criterion by which to choose *the* good life.

The theory is thus the theory of the ideal chooser – which is a fair description of the way in which utilitarianism approaches politics. But Rawls's theory is significantly different from both ideal-observer theory and utilitarianism. Utilitarianism began as ideal-observer theory in the theories of Smith and Hume but had the drawback of being vague; the opinion of the ideal observer on certain important issues is unclear. With the introduction of attempts at utility calculation (for example, in Bentham's felicific calculus) this vagueness was overcome at least in theory – but at some cost. That cost we may call the acceptance of a reductive individualism, which Rawls condemns for ignoring individual separateness. Rawls's own theory is an attempt to overcome the vagueness of ideal-observer theory and the reductionism of utilitarianism – though in the event, I shall argue, the failings of both are preserved, albeit in different forms.

The vagueness of ideal-observer theory is partly a consequence of the failure to define adequately the proper object of concern. Consider the characterization of Hume's view of moral principles as generalizations about the promotion of social utility.[30] This may *seem* clear enough when applied to large-scale political systems like conservatism or liberalism, which can be presented as resting on disagreements about the utility of different economic and social systems – in effect, disagreement over which system delivers the (most) goods. But say we try to apply this form of reasoning to a smaller-scale issue like the morality of abortion. We have no guidance on this issue since as yet we have not been told what counts as a relevant consideration. In particular, is the fetus a proper object of concern? The theory as so far specified is inadequate to the task. Even the success with large-scale phenomena is revealed as spurious, since the obvious basis of calculation, the interests of a human being, has not been either specified or defended.

Now satisfaction utilitarianism is an attempt to avoid this defect by providing itself with an adequately defined maximand. In assessing the value of institutions, actions and so on we are to consider the actual or likely states of mind of those who are, will be, or are likely to be affected. Only the states of mind, or states of feeling, of persons (or, in some theories, of sentient creatures) are to be considered.

Rawls condemns utilitarianism, in effect, because of what it posits as a basic object of concern. But since an adequately defined object of concern is crucial to decidability – and ultimately to any determinate output from the original position – Rawls must offer an alternative. That alternative is, of course, the self-concern of the 'self' of liberal economic theory, but what exactly is this self and what does its self-concern amount to?

By making the concern centre on primary goods to be used in the execution of plans of life Rawls seems to have inflated the notion of individualism somewhat. The concern seems to be about persons, their plans and projects. But because the concern is the concern of an egoist behind a veil of ignorance, the concern is with preserving options regarding various conceptions of the good life. The inexactitude of this is apparent. On one interpretation, which we may call Kantian, it means that the ultimate bearer of value is not the individual, his life or well-being; rather it is reduced from this to his freedom of choice. This is another form of reductionism and, as I shall argue in the next chapter, it has untenable consequences for political philosophy. On another interpretation, suggested by the theory of mind involved in the characterization of the people in the original position, the object of concern begins to resemble that of utilitarianism. Ignorant as to his own particular conception of the good life, a person in the original position is likely to opt for the lowest common denominator in the good life. He may think of these as primary goods, but in essence the concern is with desire satisfaction – for whatever a good life involves it will involve that. The theory is in danger of collapsing back into utilitarianism – by default.

But worse, because it leaves us with no useful theory at all, is the defect of vagueness. In characterizing the choosers as rational egoists abstracted from their own view of the good life, Rawls is sidestepping the central issue of what should be the object of concern. To be sure we have some idea of the preferences of people in the original position but this omission renders the theory vague (undecidable). To take our previous example: is the fetus an object of concern for a person in the original position? Does it matter to him that he might be aborted? The self of liberal economic theory has no opinion on this because he is too abstract. So the theory is incomplete.

And once we see that the choices of people in the original position are vague on this issue because of vagueness over the object of concern, we can see that this undermines the certainty of their more obvious choices. When we demand to know the nature of the proper object of concern it dissolves in front of us, undermining all the output of the original position. For if we do not know what really matters (for example, whether the pre-natal dying could be considered the worst-off group) we can make no choices. People in the original position are simply confused. Thus the defects of both ideal-observer theory and utilitarianism are incorporated into Rawls's system.

I have tried to identify a range of defects in the Rawlsian methodology – the ungrounded incorporation of philosophical liberalism, the failure of his deontology and, in general, the tendency to end up with the worst aspects of several theories as a result of trying to distil the best from each. The most serious charge, I think, is that Rawls has no way of convincing anyone who does not share the presuppositions of his method – and this is hardly a satisfactory result.

Rawls, however, has yet another device in his repertoire which may seem to offer a reply to the charge that he has failed to deal adequately with relativism. This is the notion of reflective equilibrium. The original position, I have argued, embodies liberalism. It is also meant to embody the constraints implicit in ordinary moral thought. Thus it seems that ordinary moral thought must be liberal. It is to this curious view, that when we view morals and politics from 'the perspective of eternity'[31] the tenets of liberalism are confirmed, that I now turn.

REFLECTIVE EQUILIBRIUM

The core of Rawls's moral methodology is the device of reflective equilibrium. When faced with rival theories, conflicting judgements or beliefs, we can employ this technique to produce a systematic general theory of moral doctrine. Rawls begins with this claim:

> **There is a definite if limited class of facts against which conjectured principles can be checked, namely, our considered judgements in reflective equilibrium.**[32]

The idea is that we begin with particular moral intuitions or opinions, confirm that we are sincere in holding them, and, in attempting to systematize them, make explicit the general principles which lie behind them. We move back and forth from the general to the particular, amending economically, until we form a coherent structure of judgements.

Rawls, however, seems to have two distinct conceptions of this procedure. The first asserts that the process is completely dialectical so that we can trade off both opinions and principles (what counts is not just considered judgements but considered judgements in *reflective equilibrium*) – nothing, in theory, is exempt from revision. The second recognizes a sub-class of initial opinions which are to be seen as fixed points around which all else must be accommodated.

There is good reason for this equivocation, but whichever interpretation is adopted we still need a reason to adopt this approach at all. One reason for constructing theory by this trade-off process is the need for coherence in practical theory. It helps in deciding what to do if we have a set of considerations which inform our choice in a consistent way. But there could be many such systems (and all practical philosophies claim to be such). So how can we tell which system to adopt? In using reflective equilibrium, how do we determine which intuitions are to count (for we must assume that they cannot all be accommodated)? As with belief in general, coherence is only useful if we have some way of independently checking, say, the starting point – by observation, for example. In the case of moral judgements we have no reason to think that strongly held intuitions correspond to some bedrock of justification for we have not yet been told what moral judgements are.

Thus the coherence/intuitionist position requires some meta-ethical support. Rawls attempts to be neutral amongst meta-ethical theories although he is clearly committed to objectivity in morals. Dworkin takes a step towards providing such a theory and at the same time resolving Rawls's dilemma over which version of reflective equilibrium to adopt by introducing a distinction between 'natural' and 'constructive' interpretations.[33] He advocates the latter as the only way to account for two-way revisability, whereas the former is rejected on the grounds that it mistakes moral judgements as similar in form to basic observations in science. This view of moral judgements is quite wrong, according to Dworkin, and we can therefore ignore particular intuitions without violating any basic truth. Still, intuition is the basis of any morality and hence any moral theory, though our object is only 'to fit the particular judgements on which [we] act into a coherent programme of action'.[34]

But this is surely to ignore Rawls's reason for alluding to the fixed-point version of reflective equilibrium. The dialectical version, favoured by Dworkin, deprives moral theory of any sure and unchallengeable ground – as Dworkin admits, 'The test concededly will yield different results for different groups and for the same group at different times, as the common ground of confident intuition shifts.'[35] This more or less upholds relativism, something Rawls rejects. Yet he in turn can offer no methodological basis for treating some intuitions as more basic than others. Intuition as such is the basis of the theory and if a systematic result is to be produced, it must be on the basis of everyone agreeing on which intuitions to include at the beginning. This, to say the least, is not that impressive a mode of philosophical argument. If everyone agrees in the first place there is very little to argue about.

Thus Dworkin is exactly wrong. Political philosophy of the kind Rawls practises cannot rely on coherence theories unless these rest on fixed points which perform the same function as basic statements do in scientific inquiry; otherwise there is no answer to relativism. Yet Rawls's fixed-point version of reflective equilibrium rests on an already existing consensus which only exists, if at all, in modern Western cultures. Again relativism goes unchallenged. For example, Rawls thinks the notion of fairness is the overarching idea in moral reasoning. Many would agree that this is so, yet challenge him over his essentially liberal notion of fairness – it is not an Old Testament or Aristotelian notion since it ignores desert.

We can see the deficiencies in Rawls's approach by examining the views of those philosophers he himself takes to be his precursors, namely Aristotle and Kant. Both of these thinkers held in respect, though for different reasons, the opinions of the many or, as Kant called it, the 'moral knowledge of common human reason'. They attempted to articulate the presuppositions of ordinary moral thought in order to provide it with a philosophical foundation of which the ordinary person is unaware.

But, of course, such a project would be misconceived unless we have reason to think that ordinary moral thought has such presuppositions. Both Kant and Aristotle had such reasons. Kant's rationalism led him to assume that morality is a form of knowledge with a unitary nature, governed by a supreme principle, and that men are rational enough to grasp the less abstract part of its truth. Aristotle's naturalism led him to think that a creature is unlikely to be mistaken about its own good in straightforward circumstances, otherwise it would not survive – that is, it is natural for things to have a tendency to pursue their own *telos*. But Aristotle does not simply systematize ordinary moral thought. He was perfectly well aware of diversity on the question of the good life, and his search for fixed points as the basis of substantive ethical theory did not end in a falsely conceived consensus. Rather he perceived consensus only on the name men gave to the good life, not on its content. This problem had to be answered by philosophical reflection and Aristotle's answer to relativism centres on his doctrine of the mean.

By Kant's time much had changed with morality, yet he still proceeded as though ordinary moral thought was essentially unified, free from internal contradictions. Rawls also accepts this, yet the idea seems incredible. Our moral system, after all, is the product of different moral traditions from which the term 'moral' acquires different sorts of meaning.

If, following the advice of MacIntyre,[36] we attend to some aspects of sociology and various facts about the genesis of our moral beliefs, the appeal to intuitions takes on a rather dubious status. Our beliefs in morals are strongly influenced by the particular culture which bred us, and thus depend on history and society as well as parents, teachers, peers, media and social class. It is also clear, as Singer says, that the moral convictions we have derive 'from discarded religious systems, from warped views of sex and bodily functions, or from customs necessary for the survival of the group in social and economic circumstances that now live in the past'.[37]

Thus, without the grounding provided by Aristotle or Kant (and Rawls offers none such), reflective equilibrium as the systematization of ordinary moral thought can claim to be nothing more than a reshuffled pack of moral prejudices – an assessment supported by our examination of the rest of the theory.

As usual, however, the device of reflective equilibrium is not so easily characterized or dismissed. In discussing the derivation of the conditions of the correct initial position, Rawls claims that 'the conditions embodied in the description of the original position are ones that we do in fact accept'.[38] This, as I think is clear by now, is simply false. Accepting the possibility of this, Rawls claims that philosophical reflection may persuade us into acceptance. If this philosophical reflection is an appeal to the method of reflective equilibrium then again we must reject Rawls's claim – for that should persuade no one. But next Rawls states that 'each aspect of the contractual situation can be given supporting grounds'.[39] This again may be an appeal to reflective equilibrium but it is more likely that it asserts that there are substantive moral arguments in favour of the conditions of the original position – and indeed there are many such in the book. For example, the veil of ignorance is partly defended on the basis of the irrelevance of moral desert in the choice of principles. Clearly, however, in giving this as the structure of the argument all else changes. We proceed from the argument that judgements based on moral desert are irrational to the conclusion that principles of justice should ignore them. But now we have no mention (or need) of social contracts or of reflective equilibrium, merely the normal structure of philosophical reflection and argument. And this leads to the conclusion that the methodological devices employed by Rawls are at best irrelevant and more likely destructive of any sound philosophical construction.

JUSTIFICATION: FURTHER CONSIDERATIONS

1. The Kantian Interpretation

It is often suggested that if all else fails (and ultimately, I suggest, this means the method of reflective equilibrium) then what Rawls calls 'the Kantian interpretation of the original position' can be developed into a Kantian-based theory of justice and Rawls's system thereby saved. By the same token, there are those who condemn Rawls simply because they see him as rehashing all the old Kantian errors.

In fact, the connections between the Rawlsian system and Kant's critical method are too loose for either of these claims to be sustained. Rawls in no way endorses the Kantian moral epistemology and so neither gains nor loses from its cogency or infirmity. In saying that justice as fairness can be given a Kantian interpretation, Rawls only intends to say that many of the central considerations which lend appeal to Kant's moral theory can be seen to be instantiated in the original position. The vital Kantian notions, in Rawls's view, are those of autonomy and the categorical imperative and so he claims that 'The original position may be viewed, then, as a procedural interpretation of Kant's conception of autonomy and the categorical imperative.'[40] This is not, I emphasize, the claim that the conditions of the original position can be derived from the same source as that which Kant thought supported these central notions (that is, abstract rationality). It is, rather, the claim that the original position is a way of fleshing out, in a way that does no violence to the Kantian values, these central Kantian conceptions.

What Rawls is doing in this section (s. 40), as he does often, is trying to show that his own theory assimilates most of what is best in all of the major moral theories in the Western tradition (especially the liberal ones). It is essentially a promotional ploy aimed at those who consider themselves Kantian. They are to consider Rawls a friend and ally, at least in matters of substance.

For Kant, autonomy is the observance of self-legislated principles or maxims of action. It is to be distinguished from acting on mere whim or inclination, these being aspects of the non-rational (and for Kant amoral) part of our nature. But it is also to be distinguished from principled action based solely on our sensual nature (such as the principle of self-interest based on hedonism) since this is heteronomous. To act autonomously is to act rationally, where this means to act on maxims which respect certain formal constraints, constraints derived from the nature of rationality itself. These constraints are called 'categorical imperatives' and find their ultimate expression in the various formulations of the 'Categorical Imperative', the first of which is: 'Act so that the maxim of your action can be willed as a universal law.'[41]

Rawls feels that the original position is faithful to these demands. Because the people therein are to choose or legislate behind the veil of ignorance they are legislating in abstraction from particular desires and interests, basing their concern on beings possessed of desires and interests as such. The veil of ignorance converts an egoist into a universal legislator by forcing him to consider everyone's interests as potentially his own. In legislating in abstraction from particular concerns and adopting a universal, impartial standpoint, Rawls thinks his people observe the Kantian strictures.

How far this is true is doubtful. We may wonder, for example, whether the concern of people in the original position, based as it is on a desire to maximize their share of primary goods in real life, could ever be made consistent with the Kantian ethos – it rules out the notion of desert, for example, and this is something central to Kant's substantive ethics. Responsibility is at the core of the foundation of Kant's entire theory – the ascription of free will to human beings.

We can leave it to Kantian scholars to determine how compatible the two approaches are. For our concern here is with the issue of any possible support the Kantian system may afford. Of course, this requires that the systems *be* compatible. But more is also required. First, it must be the case that the Kantian theory somehow goes 'deeper' than the justifications so far considered in support of Rawls's system. Second, we must be able to derive the Rawlsian conclusions from the Kantian base without resort to extraneous considerations – for to do so renders the theory non-Kantian.

However, Rawls himself is in no doubt that his theory is divorced from Kantianism in just these ways. First, although

Kant attempts to provide depth to his moral philosophy by trying to ground ethics in (abstract) practical reasoning, Rawls denies the possibility of so doing.

> **Kant did not show that acting from the moral law expresses our nature in identifiable ways that acting from contrary principles does not.**[42]

This is a version of the familiar objection, going back at least to Hegel, that Kant's formalism is an empty affair. From the formal constraints of rationality alone nothing in particular follows (save consistency). Thus Rawls eschews this Kantian basis for his moral epistemology.

On the second requirement Rawls is clear that the derivation of his principles relies on much more than the formal constraints of right. The conditions of the original position are much fuller than those of rationality – for example, the theory of primary goods requires knowledge of human preferences to the extent that these goods are seen as universally useful means.

Thus the formalism of Kant's rationalism is seen by Rawls as a useless moral epistemology. Thus there can, for Rawls, be no Kantian justification (as opposed to interpretation) of the original position. Rather, we return to the contention of Rawls that his theory is an alternative (and superior) method to that of Kant and yet captures the essence of the Kantian values.

2. *The Argument by Elimination*

Rawls has several proposals concerning ultimate issues of justification in moral theory. He begins by rejecting two common approaches, the 'Cartesian', which attempts to construct a moral system from self-evident axioms (like Euclid's geometry), and the 'naturalist', which defines value terms with reference to natural properties (as some utilitarians define 'good' in terms of pleasure) and validates its judgements using ordinary evidence.

> **I have not proceeded as if first principles, or conditions thereon, or definitions either, have special features that permit them a peculiar place in justifying a moral doctrine.**[43]

Instead, 'justification is a matter of the mutual support of many considerations, of everything fitting together into one coherent view'.[44] And this means, Rawls thinks, 'to regard a moral theory just as any other theory'.[45]

The essence of this 'coherence' view is, of course, the theory of reflective equilibrium. In stating the doctrine in this broad form Rawls is explicitly inviting a structural comparison with other (successful) theories, with natural science for example. As we have seen, there is no warrant for treating moral beliefs in moral theory like observations in scientific theory, but there is also another error involved here, an error having to do with the scope ascribed to morality in practical affairs.

For Rawls, final justification rests on the claim that justice as fairness is a coherent view of considered moral beliefs when compared to rival *moral* conceptions. The theory is the best history has to offer, the best available from the range of moral theories on offer. But moral theories do not exhaust the set of practical philosophies. In order that the justification of a moral theory be anything like that of a scientific theory we have to be able to say that moral beliefs are in the same category as factual observations. Without getting into the debate about just what status a moral belief has, it seems we can deny that this is so. For we are not comparing like with like. Moral theories do not simply compete with other moral theories, they compete with all practical philosophies. In thinking that the moral (like nature, for example) is a realm alone Rawls is making a category error. There are immoral and amoral practical philosophies and if we use considered *practical* beliefs in the process of reflective equilibrium then justice as fairness is an unlikely result. Morality is a much smaller part of our practical concerns than many moral philosophers imagine.

Whatever else, Rawls is refreshingly candid about the final status of his theory. He more or less admits that the theory is false or inadequate. For although Rawls rejects the charge of relativism he accepts that we may produce an alternative characterization of the original position so that the principles chosen may be different. This will, however, be progress towards a better theory. The position maintained is therefore objective and fallible.

Accordingly, Rawls's ultimate defence of his theory is the negative case he propounds in the rejection of its main rivals. Although justice as fairness is almost certainly a false theory it is the best available – and this is a reason to accept it. Rawls claims that 'The only thing that permits us to acquiesce in an erroneous theory is the lack of a better one.'[46] It is, it seems, a sufficient condition for accepting a theory that it is the best one available – even when it is known to be false. Perhaps this has a certain plausibility in the realm of natural science. Consider, for example, the irrationality of ignoring the Newtonian picture of the universe just because it was known not to hold of certain situations. It became rational to give up the Newtonian model only when a better one was devised (by Einstein). Rawls thinks the same is true in moral theory – that utilitarianism once held the field but can now be discarded in favour of justice as fairness. But as we have seen, there is good reason to doubt this analogy between scientific and moral theories. Crucially we need good reason to accept *any* moral theory. If a moral theory is false and we have reason to be suspicious of moral theory as such (and there are many such reasons) then we surely have good grounds for dismissing the claim that the best moral theory available is to be accepted. Again the correct analogy is with practical theories in general, not just those that could be considered moral.

Of course many of us will accept the premiss that some moral theory must be true. Why we believe this is something we may wish to leave aside for the moment (though it is of course essential to any fully justified theory). How cogent a case does Rawls present on this basis? Is his theory the best of a 'bad lot'?

Rawls identifies three main rivals to justice as fairness – intuitionism, utilitarianism and perfectionism. Let us look at each in turn.

Intuitionism, as Rawls defines it, is the view that there is a plurality of fundamental principles of right action. Such a view is untenable, he thinks, as it suffers from two crippling defects – the one practical, the other epistemological. Intuitionism in structure is associated with Cartesianism in moral epistemology. Basic principles of action are identified through being self-evident to our moral intuitive faculty (sometimes thought of as a moral sense). Rawls denies the possibility of such knowledge. The practical problem is that the plurality of principles may dictate conflicting actions when they bear on the same situation. This lack of coherence and consistency leaves us with a practical indeterminacy. This is to say that practical reason cannot reach the level of architectonics.

Clearly we would prefer to have a theory which avoids these practical problems if possible. How, though, do we know that one is possible? Rawls may claim to have produced one but he has done so in a deeply question-begging way. The basic methodological device of reflective equilibrium simply assumes that a coherent, decidable theory is possible. Any moral beliefs we have which would stand in the way of this system have to be ignored or distorted. But Rawls has given no reason to support his view that morality is ultimately coherent.

We must agree, though, that Cartesianism is a hopelessly optimistic approach to morals. Our intuition is simply unable to furnish us with the requisite principles. However, may not our intuition provide us with other useful data? Indeed, does Rawls himself not rely on the intuitive deliverances of our considered moral judgements? If that ground is seen to fail there is another object for intuition: the nature of the good for man.[47] Rawls has little to say against this kind of 'intuitionism'.

Rawls's case against *utilitarianism* is similarly incomplete. His central complaint is that utilitarianism adopts 'for society as a whole the principle of rational choice for one man'.[48] That principle is to maximize the sum of satisfaction of (rational) desires. It is rational (though not necessarily moral) for the individual to 'adopt that plan which maximizes the expected net balance of satisfaction'.[49] When this is employed as a social principle, however, the distinction between persons is lost – for only satisfactions as such are the concern. This, Rawls says, is unjust. 'Justice denies that the loss of freedom for some is made right by a greater good shared by others.'[50] If we care only about satisfactions it is at least theoretically possible to sanction the institution of slavery – in a situation where the slaves would not be much worse off than otherwise but the masters would be if slavery were not sanctioned.

Whatever the demerits of slavery in such a situation Rawls's grounds for rejecting it seem unsound. For if it is conceded that egoism is rational for the individual there seem to be only two possible attitudes to morality. First, and most obviously, it may be seen as a false body of belief, something society foists on us to prevent our wholeheartedly pursuing our own interests. This will block any attempt to construct a binding morality. Second, we may abstract the object of concern (satisfaction of desires) from the selves to whom they belong and treat these as the ultimate value. This is to say that what makes egoism rational from one point of view (that of the isolated individual) also makes utilitarianism rational from a 'universal' point of view.

Rawls's attempt to reject utilitarianism founders because he has not gone beyond the utilitarian theory of the good. He relies on the same theory of the good while trying to subordinate it to his conception of justice. Not only is that theory of justice a groundless imposition, it is now seen to be clearly irrational. The utilitarian theory of the good tells us not just what is good, but also that any moral constraint (like justice) must be derived from it; that, at least, is the import of basing practical reason on that theory of value. So Rawls is trying to wed contradictory approaches to the notion of justice.

When we turn to the case of *perfectionism* Rawls is similarly unconvincing. Perfectionism is the view that society ought to be organized so as to promote human excellence – whatever that is seen to comprise; art and science flourishing, for example. But Rawls rejects this on the basis of his thin theory of the good. Technically, people in the original position reject a perfectionist principle since they are concerned solely with their share of primary goods. They prefer to have the greatest equal liberty consistent with a similar liberty for others.

Rawls does not contend 'that the criteria of excellence lack a rational basis' and admits that 'comparisons of intrinsic value can obviously be made'.[51] However, although 'justice as fairness allows that in a well-ordered society the values of excellence are recognized, the human perfections are to be pursued within the limits of the principle of free association'.[52]

Rawls is saying that although we have viable notions of excellence in the various fields of human practice these are to be subordinated to the freedom an individual must have in choosing his way of life: 'The state may not coerce people or offer incentives (in the way of distributive shared) in order to promote activities of more intrinsic value.'[53]

How is this justified? For Rawls it is because the conditions of the original position rule it out. But this is circular. The original position is a rival to perfectionism, so must offer independent criticisms. It is the advocate of perfectionism who is to be persuaded to accept the conditions of the original position as correct. Rawls only hints at reasons here: perfectionism tends, for example, to élitism and the denial of individual liberty. However, it is unclear why these are criticisms of the perfectionist advocate of élitism or totalitarianism. One's fear of a system is not a sufficient ground for refusing to debate its case on equal terms. In any case, there are clearly examples of perfectionist liberal theories, where man finds his true potential only through the exercise of his free choice (J. S. Mill is an example).

What Rawls seeks to do is to impose a kind of democracy on the way a conception of the good may operate. Everyone has to be convinced that social arrangements are as good for him as they can be, as he himself perceives his good. As one theorist asks in the same spirit, 'What could be better for a person than his own development of a plan of life that seems to him good?'[54] Possibly, it may be replied, to simply follow a plan of life which is in fact good. If a determinate conception of the good is available, Rawls's concentration on individual autonomy becomes merely a fetish. Why burden people with a freedom that may on occasion be bad for them?

As an argument by elimination Rawls's case is hardly convincing. Not only does he fail to eliminate his rivals but he also admits that his list of options is not exhaustive. It would seem, then, that our attempt to find some ultimate ground of justification for justice as fairness has run out of steam. In the end Rawls's theory is merely a castle in the air – albeit for some a very elegant castle.

4.

ROBERT NOZICK
AND THE ENTITLEMENT THEORY
OF JUSTICE

There is a view of the well-ordered society which is called libertarian. This is a purer form of liberalism than social democracy, in that it isolates the value of individual liberty from those of welfare and equality. Using this sole value it attempts to formulate rules concerning what individuals may do to one another, what they may do in the way of organizing the state and what powers that state may have. The individual, with whom we begin, is to have a definite sphere of unfettered activity (or inactivity) where for anyone to interfere, and this includes the state, is to commit a wrong.

Characteristically this sphere of influence corresponds to the powers conferred on individuals by capitalist or free-enterprise economies. The individual has the formal power to acquire property, to trade it, to hire the labour power of others or sell his own. He may acquire great wealth or struggle in poverty – all as his ability, effort and luck would have it. The state, for its part, may only service this system. It may act and punish to prevent the use of force (murder, robbery and so on) and fraud, but it may not tax or confiscate property in order to help the needy or undertake great public works. The poor must help themselves or rely on charity. For those so inclined and wealthy enough, health insurance and pension contributions will reduce the risk of falling on hard times – but any collective endeavour beyond protecting persons and their rightful activities must be left solely to voluntary clubs and associations.

There exist various attempts to justify this model of proper social organization – for example, Adam Smith and, more recently, Milton Friedman offer what amount to utilitarian justifications: the system is justified because it is so productive that everyone will end up better off. But because of the implausibility of this claim (utilitarianism is better served by more egalitarian systems) libertarians seek a more secure foundation.

Nozick offers just such a foundation in a particular conception of individual (moral or natural) rights. When it is recognized that people have certain rights then it will also be clear that the 'minimal state' described above is the best (only) way to secure those rights and that any more powerful state will actually violate those rights unless it rests on the unanimous consent of its members (for people have the option to waive their rights). The minimal state is thus preferable to anarchy (for there people's rights are less securely protected) and more likely to be justified than the redistributive state (for it is unlikely that everyone will agree to that). Obviously only certain rights would have the properties Nozick requires. A right to help when in need is out of the question, for example. So what rights do we have?

A person may exercise total control over himself and his possessions (that is, buy and sell, abuse or destroy, donate or bequeath) so long as he does not interfere with the freedom of others to do likewise. Where a person or his rightful freedom is abused he may exact a due reparation and punishment.

These powers are described as moral rights and are presented as fundamental to political life, indeed to morality (or politically relevant morality) itself for they are not derived from any goal (like the maximizing of utility) or any value (like fairness or even freedom). Further, these rights are said to be 'side-constraints' on action where this means that the violation of a moral right is a wrong which cannot be justified even if it prevents greater wrong or promotes great good. Similarly, there is no question of trade-off. The rights of some may not be violated in order to protect the rights of others. The observance of rights is not a goal to be maximized.

Nozick's strategy is straightforward. He identifies two rivals to his view of the well-ordered society and seeks to demonstrate their moral inferiority. These are the stateless society (anarchy) and the more than minimal state, the state with redistributive or goal-setting powers. It is to the case for the minimal state that we now turn.

THE DICTATES OF THE RIGHTS THESIS

The social order (or disorder) known as anarchy, wherein no coercive relations are permitted, is the condition Nozick selects as his 'rest-position' – a situation from which we may move only by morally permissible means. This starting point and its concomitants (of inviolable freedom of the person and the absolute right to property in the self and its possessions) is largely taken for granted – which at this stage is allowable since Nozick is arguing with people who endorse his starting point (that is, anarchists). Rights are expressions of 'natural freedom' and anarchy is seen as the obvious instantiation of this. Nozick is trying to show that anarchy can be replaced by the minimal state without violating anarchist legitimacy.[1] It is acccepted, then, that the voluntary consent of persons is a necessary condition of any move away from anarchy towards the state.

Anarchists themselves see any such move towards coercive institutions as immoral, irrational and unnecessary: there are no serious problems in their 'state of nature'. Less optimistic thinkers have proposed grounds which make the move towards the state both rational and necessary (for survival, for example).[2] However, to be morally acceptable this move must rest on consent and clearly not all men are rational enough to give it. The ploy of social-contract theory of appealing to hypothetical or tacit consent is seen as inadequate since without an express waiver on the part of everyone concerned all natural rights must be respected.

The novelty of Nozick's approach, which is intended to sidestep these and other problems associated with express-consent theories, is an attempt to explain how a state can emerge from the state of nature without violating anyone's rights (or almost) yet without resort to a social contract. The state, Nozick argues, can be the unintended outcome of other-directed actions (in essence, voluntary exchanges). What the argument becomes is an *explanation* of how rational, self-interested parties will interact in such a way as to produce the state without violating the rules which govern proper interaction. No one intends that the state should emerge; it does so by an 'invisible hand' process. Importantly, this explanation turns out to be a *justification* because it involves only legitimate processes emanating from a legitimate origin. The notion of an invisible hand is only a metaphor to indicate that an apparently planned result can arise via haphazard processes. Consider, for example, the process of evolution, which many are unable to conceive of as undesigned (by the invisible hand of God) yet which science accounts for satisfactorily in other terms. Similarly, economists make reference to an invisible hand to 'explain' the tendency of supply and demand to equilibrium in a free market when of course their real efforts at explanation rely on micro-economic behaviour.

Nozick follows Locke[3] in locating the central problem of the state of nature as the violation of rights, either directly or indirectly through over-zealous punishment. Relying on the notion of efficiency in the division of labour Nozick argues that enterprising individuals will set up business as bodyguards and agents of reparation and punishment, acting as their clients' agents in these matters and calling themselves 'protection agencies'.

Now although advocates of free enterprise normally prefer many suppliers of a service or commodity (since this helps rule out coercion and profiteering in the market) Nozick actually welcomes the trend to monopoly in this particular area. There are many advantages in having just one, all-pervading protection agency – the biggest, in essence, will offer the most security. It is this agency that will become, in time, the minimal state. Before seeing how, though, we should ask a question. Is it rational to join or hire such an agency? Remember that individuals in the state of nature will hire only out of a concern that their rights be protected. Would they not perceive a great danger in a large private police force, the obvious danger that by whim it could simply become a tyrannical *de facto* state? And would they not then seek to maintain a plurality of suppliers by leaving one agency when it seemed to be getting too large? People might fear what such an agency might become so that they would refuse, *en masse*, to hire it. The threat of the total subordination of their rights has to be weighed against the reality of rights-violation in the state of nature. Is this bad enough to run the risk of creating a Leviathan?

The next move by the dominant protective agency may confirm a sceptic's worst fears. The agency is not yet a state because it does not claim a monopoly of the legitimate use of force in its territory; nor does it extend its protection to all its residents. There may be people who have not joined it and who reserve the right to use force when their rights are violated. The agency does not like this, for it has 'a strong tendency ... to deem all other procedures (than its own), or even the "same" procedures run by others, either unreliable or unfair'.[4] Accordingly, in order to safeguard its own clients the agency issues recalcitrants with an offer they cannot refuse. In the final analysis it forces its services on everyone and forces them all to pay for them. It could not do otherwise because if people saw that you could get the service for nothing, then they would all try to opt out of paying and the agency (and thus the state) would collapse. The 'offer' is described by Nozick as compensation by the agency for transgressing the rights of non-clients (through not permitting them to enforce criminal justice themselves). Thus it seems that the violation of rights may be necessary after all if the state is to emerge. But this is justified, thinks Nozick, because to permit freedom here is to risk harm to clients (through unfair punishments of their offences) and because the wrong is immediately compensated.

Notice, however, that apart from this violation there may be another. This is so if someone does not want 'compensation'. Forcing someone to accept something is a violation of his rights. A gift has to be voluntarily accepted. Now a person may have good reason for refusing the service 'offered' by the protective agency if he associates danger with the monopoly of supply. The minimal state, in this eventuality, could only exist by continually violating the rights of such people and would then be illegitimate. Are there any such people, however? The rationality of their rejection depends, of course, on their perception of the relative dangers of the state and the state of nature. According to Nozick we can assume that people in the state of nature behave morally for the most part; and Locke, whose state of nature this is, generally regards offence against natural law in the state of nature as an inconvenience rather than as a war of all against all. In further support we could ask how many states have so limited themselves that we could reassure the Lockean anarchist on this point?

If the minimal state is problematic then we can be sure that the more than minimal state is unreachable by the same route. Any state that does more than enforce the terms of freely entered contracts and protect its members against force, theft and fraud will necessarily violate some people's rights (that is, the rights of those who do not consent to it – most likely the rich and powerful). This is a simple result of ascribing to men Nozick's notion of natural freedom.

By natural freedom is meant the possession of certain 'negative' rights – rights against others interfering coercively in our affairs and the right to property. This might be contrasted with a notion of 'social freedom', which would attribute to persons certain positive rights – rights seen as moral claims on others to provide for us, for example a claim against the state to provide for welfare or education. Nozick simply denies that we have such positive rights, though his grounds for doing so are unclear. Ultimately we require some explanation of the grounds of rights in general but Nozick postpones an inquiry into the moral basis of his position and settles instead for descriptions of moral test cases which are designed to elicit our intuitive support for his own approach and to undermine the appeal of rival theories. However, the notion of respect for persons, derived from Kant, is given prominence. We are to 'act so as to treat humanity both in oneself and others always as an end and never merely as a means'. This idea is intended to rule out several things. Nozick thinks that it proscribes utilitarianism (where some may be used merely to promote the welfare of others); paternalism (where someone may be used solely as a means to his own, unwanted welfare) and Rawls's theory of justice, especially the Principle of Difference (where people's talents and property may be used as a means to benefit the worst-off group). It is clear, however, that this reference to Kant is not intended to reveal the true basis of Nozick's moral philosophy. We are not being asked to accept the Kantian moral epistemology, merely to be impressed by its intuitively appealing output.

The rejection of any state more powerful than the night-watchman variety is implicit in the rights Nozick ascribes to individuals. More particularly, it is a simple corollary of the acceptance of those rights as foundational to any politically relevant morality that any conception of justice which prescribes redistribution of wealth or proscribes certain activities (like the amassing of great personal wealth) must be rejected. For the state to employ such practices it must continuously violate people's rights; it must, for example, prohibit capitalist acts between consenting adults.

This, of course, is no surprise, given the infinite value ascribed to natural freedom in the political realm. Nozick's only innovation here is a general classificatory scheme for conceptions of social justice and his attempt to reveal quite general defects in every conception but his own. Principles of justice, Nozick explains, are most revealingly characterized in terms of considerations of history, of end-states, or of patterns.

A *historical* principle of justice is one which makes the justice of a distribution depend on how it came about. Under such a dispensation a person's past actions and situation may create differential entitlements or deserts to things. An *end-state* principle of justice is one which makes the justice of a distribution depend on the conformity of a state of affairs to some structure or goal. A *patterned* principle of justice is one which makes the justice of a distribution depend on some specific historical factor, some characteristic of individuals such as moral worth, talent or industriousness.

Rawls's Difference Principle is an example of an end-state principle, since it is concerned only with an overall structural result – that the welfare of the worst-off is maximized. So too are the various utilitarian theories. This conception of justice is unacceptable, Nozick argues, because it presents justice as indifferent to personal fates. An individual's fate only matters directly as it conforms or not to the preferred structure, yet clearly it is a matter of justice that a particular person is where he is in a given distribution. An indirect concern – that he is where he is because this is the most efficient way of creating or maintaining the structure – is not enough.

A patterned principle could correct this defect if it assigns positions (goods or holdings) according to a personal attribute (when this is its ultimate reason for doing so), for example, by distributing according to individual merit or desert. But such a patterned principle is objectionable, Nozick asserts, because it seeks to impose an ideal history; because it has to correct the vagaries of real history. In so doing it will have to ignore and violate legitimate holdings – for we can legitimately acquire things otherwise than as the pattern dictates. Such patterns would be upset by the operation of luck, or the practice of gift-giving. And because we have a right to use our property as we like, any pattern is a restriction or worse on our liberty. It is therefore illegitimate.

We are left, by elimination, with justice characterized as historical but unpatterned. This is no surprise since this is merely a re-description of the natural-rights doctrine espoused by Nozick. Our rights prevent the legitimizing of the maintenance of any pattern of the pursuit of any end-state. Nozick calls his unpatterned, historical view the entitlement theory, and identifies three main components:

1. A principle of initial acquisition of holdings: we own our own bodies and its abilities and we can come to own various external objects.

2. A principle of transfer of holdings: we can trade or give away the things we own.

3. A principle of rectification: we must remedy unjust acts; for example, acts of theft or of illegitimate initial acquisition.

In essence, any distribution of holdings that results from legitimate transactions concerning legitimately acquired holdings is itself legitimate – and thus may not be interfered with on grounds of justice. In fact, to interfere (say by taxing the rich to help the needy) is unjust. The result of observing these principles should be fairly clear – we should operate an unfettered capitalist economy. Unfortunately, Nozick thinks, this is not clear. It is not clear because such a system is legitimate only if all holdings were originally acquired in the proper way. Whatever the proper way is, and this too is unclear, it is clear that much original acquisition was, and is, improper.

Of course time itself would seem to be a great legitimizer. We tend to forget that our wealthy families descend in the main from robbers, murderers and warlords. It is this tendency that motivates Marx in *Capital* to criticize capitalism in its own terms. He is at great pains to reveal as myths or nursery tales the idea that the working class descends from 'lazy rascals, spending their substance and more in riotous living', while the capitalist's forebears were a 'diligent, intelligent and above all frugal élite'. On the contrary, Marx observes, 'it is a notorious fact that conquest, enslavement, robbery, murder, in short force, play the greatest part'. 'Capital comes dripping from head to toe, from every pore, with blood and dirt.'[5]

Nozick also rejects the idyllic history presupposed by some apologists of capitalism. Any simple move to an unfettered capitalist system is rejected because present holdings are largely unjust, being derived from acts of unjust initial acquisition. Further, he rejects any pragmatic defence of the status quo in holdings because any injustice must be rectified. Nozick advocates capitalism only in an ideal situation, ideal in that all holdings have been legitimately acquired (*ab initio*) and that improper acquisitions and transfers have been rectified. This is the world where Wilt Chamberlain may trade his exceptional skills in a free market for a fortune, where the state may not interfere with holdings save to maintain it minimal functions, where the unlucky, the infirm and the incompetent have to rely on the charity of the rich to survive.

Perhaps more of us could accept Nozick's competitive society if it were a fairer one. That is to say, in the common metaphor, if everyone started in the race in the same place. This, we know, is not the case. If it were, we could expect the distribution of wealth to mirror that of 'natural' ability (that is, ability before the effects of education, etc.). The distribution of wealth would thus be approximately 'normal' (like an IQ curve) and not, as it would be under Nozick's scheme, concentrated far more in an élite than any natural ability could ever be. Obviously, in Nozick's ideal, this is because the fortunes of the parents (as well as the sins of failure and bad luck) are visited on their offspring. The accumulation of these historical contingencies leads to results many find unacceptable – people very often do not deserve their success; the resulting structure makes it very difficult for anyone to escape from the lower strata.

Even if we can accept this, there still seems to be a great difficulty concerning the care of the destitute. Perhaps leaving provision of welfare to charity would not be too objectionable (would not constitute a moral catastrophe) if charity could be relied upon. However, aside from the damage to self-respect caused by reliance on another's hand-outs there is good reason to suppose that charity would be ineffective in the alleviation of misery. The past of capitalism inspires no confidence: throughout the capitalist world it took measures by more than minimal states to begin to treat the problems of poverty. And today where welfare does depend on charity (for example, in the Third World) our record of beneficence is hardly inspiring.

In essence, we can adduce strong feelings that there exist moral considerations which count against Nozick's ideal, considerations which oppose any single-minded concern for unpatterned history and which it seems absurd to present as politically irrelevant (that is, irrelevant to what the state ought to be or ought to do). How does Nozick defend the limitations on the considerations we are to take on, how is it that we must begin only with moral rights and ignore all other moral claims? We must look to Nozick's state-of-nature theory and his theory of moral rights in order to answer this.

STATE-OF-NATURE THEORY

Critics of Nozick commonly object that the use of state-of-nature theory (with its ancillary device of invisible-hand explanations) is too limiting, that it blocks access to information, concerns or goals that are vital to any political choice. Because the minimal state has to come about unintentionally, as the result of small-scale voluntary exchanges, people cannot stand back and deliberate about what really would be the best kind of state to live in. The state is something that sneaks up on us. In this sense, it could be said that Nozick, like Rawls, imposes a veil of ignorance of people in the state of nature; though Nozick's veil of ignorance is intended to render people politically ignorant rather than personally so.

If Nozick wished to reject our criticism of his derivation of the minimal state (that people would defect from protection agencies in order to prevent one becoming dominant) on the grounds that political information is not available, then this assessment of state-of-nature theory would be sound. However, it is important to note that Nozick's use of state-of-nature theory is intended to be the very opposite of limiting. It is aimed at anarchists, who think that even the minimal state is illegitimate because it necessarily violates natural rights. Nozick uses state-of-nature theory in an attempt to demonstrate that this need not be so.

Thus state-of-nature theory plays a very specific and (to the non-anarchist) unimportant role. It plays no role at all in limiting us to the merely minimal state. As we have seen, the real limitation on setting up a state of greater power is the rights which people are said to possess. These rights entail that everyone must consent to the constitution of the more-than-minimal state – where this consent is *real*. This, however, is not to say that the use of state-of-nature theory may not create problems for Nozick's theory as a whole. There is yet another sense in which state-of-nature theory may limit the project – and that is in terms of its relevance.

There is a simple and obvious complaint against Locke that men never were in any such state of nature and that, even if they had been, no state ever did in fact arise by the process he describes (namely contract). Whether this sinks Locke, Nozick apparently avoids it because, he argues, his hypothetical history of the transition from the state of nature to civil society *need* not be describing the real origins of existing institutions or the processes which produced them. The point of such hypothetical reconstructions of the origins of a social order is to show how a political association could arise legitimately (which for Nozick means without violating rights – or almost).

It seems that Nozick thinks that if we can show how a given set of institutions could, in theory, arise legitimately, then this gives us a reason for preferring them to, or valuing them more highly than, those which could only arise via illegitimate processes. The bastard state can only remove the stigma of its origins if there is some way a state just like it could have had a legitimate birth. To show that an institution could have arisen in an approved fashion is to provide a justification of it. The state, then, cannot be justified as a necessary evil or a positive good. Such considerations are irrelevant.

There is on the face of it something dubious about this approach. The fact that we can tell fairy stories, however realistic they may be, which reveal how a given state of affairs could have come about legitimately in no way proves it did so. And if it did not, what is the relevance of the myth? Not surely that any market society run by a minimal government is all right because it has the proper structure, for that is precisely the fault in a redistributive state – its concern for patterns or end-states rather than with who is where and why in any given distribution. Given that Nozick is aware of this, what exactly is he saying? Only, it seems, that if a legitimate state exists, then that state is a minimal one. Or again that there is, in theory, the possibility of a legitimate state arising from the state of nature. This, however, has the unfortunate consequence that the legitimate state can only exist where a state of nature existed to spawn it. And thus the point of a hypothetical origin is lost.

It may be thought that this criticism is not to the point on the basis of a consideration of a parallel with the way in which we assess individual actions. Suppose, for example, that an agent does A out of selfishness or other low motivations, but that A is also shown to be what an ideal moral agent would have done. Do we not have an argument for the rightness of A, as against the goodness of the agent? Can Nozick not then claim that he has an argument for the rightness of the minimal state irrespective of its origins?

There is, however, no real parallel here. The above shows only that an individual's motivations do not define the objective rightness of an act. This may appear structurally similar to Nozick's theory if a minimal state could arise through a series of unjust acts. Would not that state then be just despite its history? Is it not objectively right regardless of any particular process of development? In Nozick's view the answer must be no. To think a minimal state just no matter how it came about is to think in terms Nozick rejects – in patterns or end-states. For Nozick the historical dimension is essential to any justification, for it is only by reference to origins, and not final structures, that justice can be defined. Thus our original criticism stands: the relevance of a hypothetical state of nature remains unclear.

The reason for this unsatisfactory outcome is Nozick's aim itself – which is not to write a political tract (as Locke had done), but to explore a set of ideas and a method. And the result of all this is that because the state of nature never did nor never will exist (it being a construction designed to engage the Lockean anarchist in debate), Nozick's theory becomes irrelevant to political philosophy. The trouble is that Nozick forgets on occasion the limited nature of his project, seeming to suggest that if we could somehow get a distribution of holdings which is in fact just (and here he alludes to Rawls's principles as being useful in a rectificatory manner)[6] then the minimal state comes into its own – by right. But of course, *ex hypothesi*, there is no way to obtain a just set of holdings save by just initial acquisition and subsequent transfer, and these, I suggest, are lost to us for ever; unless, *per impossibile* (on Nozick's motivational assumptions), everyone were to give up his 'property' voluntarily and we could begin again.

So Nozick's theory is essentially Utopian in the worst sense of that term: it has no practical relevance. Like the Garden of Eden before the Fall it can offer no insight into the problems of what we are to do here and now, since we are left ignorant of what principles are to inform our choice. The theory has application nowhere.

But it may be objected that this is a premature conclusion, since Nozick can always fall back on his theory of rectification to make his theory relevant. That Nozick must rely on rectification for relevance is, I think, undeniable; yet it is doubtful whether he would be wise to do so. This is what he has to say on the matter:

> **If a set of holdings is properly generated, there is no argument for a more extensive state based upon distributive justice ... If, however, these principles are violated, the principle of rectification comes into play. Perhaps it is best to view some patterned principles of distributive justice as rough rules of thumb meant to approximate the general results of applying the principle of rectification of injustice ... a *rough* rule of thumb for rectifying injustices might seem to be the following: organize society so as to maximize the position of whatever group ends up least well-off in the society ... These issues are very complex and are best left to a full treatment of the principle of rectification ... Although to introduce socialism as the punishment for our sins would be to go too far, past injustices might be so great as to make necessary in the short run a more extensive state in order to rectify them.** [7]

One response to Nozick might be as follows: If we set up the rectificatory institutions and live with them, come to rely on them and so on, then we have admitted having lost any ideas we had on who originally owned what (legitimately). And in setting up the redistribution we lose them for ever, for we create new titles whose basis is the convention we institute to redistribute. The more-than-minimal state would then be justifying itself on a permanent basis because it has become an essential part of the new institution of property.

Thus once the redistributive state exists the question of how it arose no longer seems important, for if this state is a good thing yet could only have come about by violating rights, are we to give it up, the damage having been done? Nozick rejects the more-than-minimal state, not because of its origins (for that was only a myth), but because of its continuing need to interfere and to violate rights. But now that ground seems doubtful because those rights become mythical.

Nozick's reliance on rectification now appears to threaten his whole enterprise. The act of rectification seems to require a utilitarian justification (or some other, equally opposed to the ethics of Nozick) in virtue of the conventional nature of the rectificatory process – if property has a conventional basis, Nozick's state of nature takes on a decidedly ideological appearance.

Possession, it is said, is nine tenths of the law. Nozick thinks that because of unjust original acquisition the present holder will have no, or little, entitlement. But it is certain that some people, faced with the prospect of redistribution, will suggest leaving things as they are. They may feel that if the original just acquisition is lost in the mists of time then we have no way of knowing how to rectify. A rough rule of thumb is no answer. Certainly people are suffering because of past injustices but people would be suffering anyway – that is the way the system works.

Nozick would reply that the crucial point is that it is the wrong people who are suffering. Injustices against forebears are being visited on the descendants and only a utilitarian would be indifferent to this. The object of the interference of rectification is to give people what would have been theirs had things gone justly *ab initio*.

Now it would seem that any suggested 'rule-of-thumb' principle of rectification, like Rawls's Difference Principle, will affect legitimate and illegitimate property-holders alike. A reasonable description of rectification, then, would be that it is a process which aims to maximize the observance of individuals' rights (in their property) by intentionally violating the rights of others as a matter of course. This looks precisely like the 'utilitarian' conception of rights which Nozick rejects in his notion of rights as side-constraints.[8] If so, we can conclude that rectification, at least in the general form of a principle of redistributive justice, is unavailable to Nozick's theory. And if that is unavailable then so too is relevance.

In essence the theory is irrelevant since we only know what particular 'rights' to property are legitimate with reference to the acts of original acquisition. The complexity (often impossibility) of this task mirrors the supposed weakness of utilitarianism in its need to predict all the consequences of a person's acts. Thus an apparent advantage of Nozick's theory, its eschewing of the need for intricate investigations and calculation, is lost. It would seem then to have few advantages left.

Thus the historical perspective inherent in state-of-nature theory turns out to be irrelevant to the project of justification. Even to those who, like Nozick, are convinced of a backward-looking morality, it reveals itself as too limiting. The need to resort to consequentialism in the search for rectification (and this in the search for relevance) is testimony to this. Similarly, Nozick's view that moral philosophy (conceived in his own narrow way) sets the limits for political philosophy is revealed for just how restricting it is. For Nozick, all the important questions are answered in the moral realm (a realm of rights as side-constraints without reference to anything political, as though morality were something which could pre-date our political interaction). The moral theory here assumed by Nozick generates its own problems in dealing with political consequences, as we have seen. Such internal contradictions, I think, signal an incoherence we shall investigate further in the second area of methodological concern, the nature of basic human rights.

THE RIGHTS THESIS EXPLORED

'Individuals have rights and there are things no person or group may do to them [without violating their rights].'[9]

How do we know that people have rights, what these rights are rights to, and what importance to ascribe to them? Nozick tries to make much of his claim about what rights people have but there are those, myself included, who would deny the existence of these rights, arguing that 'belief in them is one with belief in witches and unicorns'.[10] To forestall an obvious complaint, the denial of rights does not entail the contrary of Nozick's claim above: 'People have no rights and persons or groups may do as they please to them.' No. This denial of rights is a denial of a certain conception of rights and of the role these may play in moral and political philosophy.

To be clear what is at issue here we must distinguish between two conceptions of rights – the *derivative* and the *foundational*. An example of a derivative conception of rights is that of the utilitarian who sees rights as of secondary importance, held and respected only in virtue of, and in so far as, this promotes utility: a society which respects certain rights will have a higher level of utility than one which doesn't. To see what a foundational conception of rights is we can look to the origin of natural rights. This was in natural-law theories (laws of God or rationality) where a natural right had much the same place in the system of natural law that a legal right has in a legal system: one frames the laws and then derives what rights a person has from these (cf. Locke, s. 4: a person has a right to act and use his possessions as he likes '*within the bounds of the law of nature*'). With the demise of natural-law theory there is a tendency to ascribe rights to people regardless. These rights are not derived from natural law but ascribed to people solely in virtue of their humanity or some aspect of it (free will and rationality are very popular). These rights then become the foundation on which the rest of morality is raised. This is Nozick's approach – though rights are the ground for only one aspect of morality, its political aspect (the area of legitimately enforceable behaviour).

The notion of rights plays a key role in the teleology/deontology debate. Teleological theories generally enjoin that act whose consequences are best (in terms of some good). Deontological theories assert that we can determine the rightness of an act without reference to the value of its consequences: some things are right or wrong whatever happens. Clearly the ascription of rights to people is one version of deontology. For respect for rights may not always issue in the best consequences. Although some utilitarians would insist that their theory can give adequate respect to rights, it is the perceived failure in this that has led to a revival of the foundational, hence deontological, conception of rights. Nozick, following Rawls, thinks that any teleological theory must sacrifice individual rights for the sake of its goal. Because the use of individuals in this way is deeply offensive to our moral intuitions (rights theorists claim) we must build in constraints, in the form of rights, at the very foundations of our moral and political philosophies. To take rights seriously, it is said, we must recognize the claims of individuals to free choice over contributions to the pursuit of the goal specified by the teleological theory.

No doubt then, those who value the separateness of individuals have a *motive* to advance the rights thesis. I shall discuss the adequacy of this thesis under three headings. First, can rights play the role assigned to them in countering consequentialist considerations? Second, in the common perception of morality, are rights really to be seen as these foundational entities? Third, can the conceptual link be provided between possessing some quality and possessing the corresponding right?

The central function of rights in a deontological theory is to ensure on specifiable occasions that a person cannot be forced to do or suffer something for the sake of some good – if it is his own good then rights rule out paternalism, if it is the general good then rights rule out consequentialism in general. Rights then come into our deliberations about the effects consequential considerations may have when set against the (rights-based) claims of individuals.

To do this the weight of a right must be known – we must know when a right outweighs other considerations. The clearest thesis on this is the claim that they always do, that an individual's rights are side-constraints on action. In effect, where some goal or good conflicts with someone's right his waiver must be sought if that goal or good is to be legitimately pursued. A less strong, and hence less clear, approach would be to claim that rights are at least independent, irreducible, or *sui generis* (where these mean foundational) claims against others and demand *some* considera-tion, that is, they have some – special? – weight. They are perhaps to be overridden only to avert some catastrophe. The first view is that of rights as absolute; the second view attempts some sort of compromise between rights and consequential considerations. How are we to choose which is best?

Nozick proceeds in this vein: Consider your own body. It is intimately and uniquely yours. But on a utilitarian view this is an indirect concern, a derivative matter morally speaking. So if, for example, some part of your body (a kidney, say) could produce more utility elsewhere (transplanted into a dying worthy, say) then you ought to give it (*ceteris paribus*). Not only would this be a good thing to do (Nozick would concede that much) but you have no grounds for refusing. Nozick tries to provide such grounds in his theory of rights: you have the right, on such occasions, to be selfish, even immoral. The kind of positive contribution required by utilitarianism is left to your own choice or conscience, so that neither the state nor anyone else may take your morality into its own hands.

The doctrine of rights can thus appear reassuring to an agent faced with the apparently unlimited obligations utilitarian-ism seeks to impose. Of course the doctrine is less reassuring to those whom your rights allow you to ignore. Imagine that your blood, uniquely, has developed antibodies to a certain crippling disease which affects thousands. There is no known cure. But by taking a sample of your blood a serum can be developled which would save many. Do you have the right to withhold your property? And if you do, should it be respected?

If you insist that you have this right and that it carries enough weight to crush the claims to well-being of any number of people, then you are tending towards an absolutist view of rights. People's rights can never be legitimately violated. This is the view that permeates Nozick's *Anarchy, State and Utopia* – or seems to. There, rights make doubtful the very legitimacy of the state, render illegitimate the redistribution of wealth for the greater good, ensure the individual's freedom to ignore any and every demand made of him, save that he respect the rights of others.

I take this view of rights to be untenable. Surprisingly, Nozick agrees. Commenting on his theory of rights, he remarks that he 'imagined that teleological considerations would take over to avert "moral catastrophe", but did not specify what determines where this transition takes place'.[11] One wonders, then, what *Anarchy, State and Utopia* was all about, since that work is premised on the irrelevance of moral catastrophe to the justification (or lack of it) of the capitalist system. Surely, we can dismiss the absolutist conception – for what looks like consequentialist reasons.

If consequentialism must come into our reasoning at some point the rights theorists will want that point specified. The compromise theory will need to specify just when a right may be outweighed by consequential considerations, otherwise the point of the rights thesis is lost. That point is that rights must be respected more than a consequentialist theory would anyway – if that is, rights were not foundational.

However, here we have, I suggest, an intractable problem, for it is an example of what Rawls calls 'intuitionism'. Once consequentialist considerations are admitted, the compromise theory is open to interminable casuistry concerning just how much suffering, real or expected, sanctions overriding rights. And thus the main advantage which a rights-based theory claims over utilitarianism (its decisiveness) is lost, for we have even more complicated calculations to make. In any case, such a compromise between deontology (in rights) and teleology (in consequences) is bound to be unstable. Some will wish to stress the abnormality of bowing to consequences, others that consequences have the final say.

Moving on to our second question concerning rights: regardless of which rights thesis is held (the absolute or the compromise), rights must be seen as independent, irreducible or *sui generis* claims. This is part of what it means to say that rights are foundational. If rights are reducible to other (moral) considerations – for example, claims of need or desert – then their deontological role is undermined. Unfortunately for the rights theorists, rights seem to be reducible in just this way.

A natural way of understanding the phrase 'A has a (moral) right to X' is to translate it into something like 'There is good (moral) reason to allocate to A the freedom, power or enabling conditions to X' (A is an agent, X is some act). This means that a right is not a special (*sui generis*) moral claim, rather it is only a strong way of presenting one. Generally when I claim something as a right then I am saying that, all things considered, there is a good moral reason to respect or promote my freedom in this case. Thus a right becomes an elliptical concept for the conclusion of a moral deliberation – it cannot therefore be foundational.

Against this analysis, Dworkin insists that someone can have the right to do something that is the wrong thing for him to do.[12] Thus rights have an independent existence within the normal moral framework. An example of this might be the following. You lend me a knife on condition that I return it whenever you ask. I promise to do so. The rights theorist may say that here you have a right to the return of your knife on demand. But say you demand your knife when you are in a vengeful or suicidal mood and great harm may be done. In this case it may not be right to give you the knife but you still have a right to it.

I find it difficult to make sense of this. Clearly you can have a *legal* right to something which it would be morally wrong to observe. But if something is morally wrong, isn't it merely perverse to say you have a right to do it? Of course a (rule) utilitarian could construct a system which ascribed rights to people which were rights to do wrong – but that would only be on the basis that these rights ought to be observed because of their overall contribution to the good. But the rights thesis implausibly maintains the existence of a *sui generis* right to do wrong.

In the above example we have the assertion that a moral right is a distinctive moral claim but one which can be overridden by other considerations of a moral sort. But it is surely much more natural and economical to conceive of a promise as creating a claim based on the expectation of fulfilment relative to an assumption of normal circumstances prevailing. The promise creates a defeasible, prima-facie claim and not some moral right. This way of interpreting rights talk is all the more plausible when it is realized that advocates of the view that rights constitute an independent claim provide no way of assessing by how much a right-claim outweighs the corresponding mere ought-claim. Either rights wither away to mere oughts or all moral considerations create or become rights. Social practices such as promising and private property are a basis for claims because they are thought to be, or presented as, of great use in ameliorating the human condition.

We can plausibly construe rights as claims more basically expressed in terms of straightforward moral considerations (need, desert or merit, utility). They cannot therefore be *sui generis* claims, nor trumps against consequentialist concerns, and so cannot function as the rights theorist wishes.

This is all the more telling when we consider the problems of actually showing how rights could attach to people at all.

There are two approaches to this problem of *linkage*. First, it is baldly stated that simply because people have certain qualities then they have certain rights. Second, and more circumspectly, it is argued that because people have certain qualities it is necessary that they claim certain things as rights, and recognize the same claims by others as rights. This second is an attempt to explain *how* rights attach to people.

The problem with the first approach is that it is indefensible. Perhaps to assert an unintelligible link is being faithful to the deontological tradition but it will hardly convert anyone. Consider an example. Ronald Dworkin claims that everyone has an equal right to concern and respect.[13] He means by this that when we organize society we must not exhibit bias to aid some particular frailty (like incompetence) or to promote some conception of the good life (the life of virtue, for example). We must be neutral because the rights of individuals require it. How do we have these rights, though? People are capable of suffering and frustration and therefore have the right to concern. People are capable of framing and acting on intelligent conceptions of how to live and are therefore entitled to respect.

How people have a right to *equal* concern and respect is not stated. We might suspect this is because people have an *equal* capacity for suffering, feeling frustrated, planning and executing intelligent life-plans. But this is implausible. Our capacities in all these respects vary. So then should our rights. Even if we modify the theory so that we have a right to concern and respect *proportional* to our requisite capacities, the theory still looks odd. For why should someone who is not actually or in imminent danger of suffering have the right to my concern? and why should someone who has not in reality framed and executed an intelligent life-plan have a right to my respect? If concern and respect are to be directed to failure and success (as surely they must) then we must have criteria to identify these. And it is surely impossible to identify any such criteria which are meaningful and at the same time catholic enough to give the liberal results Dworkin wants. Can we imagine that everyone is living equally intelligent lives, in some sense of intelligent?

The real problem facing such an approach, however, is this. How do we pick the qualities which are meant to provide a basis for the rights? Someone could equally well claim that people have the capacity for choice and therefore have the right to choose, and so endorse Nozick's conception of justice: 'To each as they are chosen, from each as they choose.'[14]

In determining how people ought to be treated we could appeal to many characteristics but for this appeal to transcend the arbitrary (you can, seemingly, choose what you like) we must go beyond the mere juxtaposition of capacity and right. The most obvious way to do this is to observe that certain capacities reflect certain human goods – for Dworkin's candidates, goods having to do with the satisfactions of our desires to avoid pain and frustration and to pursue goals successfully. Of course this move undermines the rights thesis – we are to treat people in certain ways because this has good consequences.

Another way is to adopt the second strategy above.

A notable recent contribution to explaining how persons have foundational rights comes from Alan Gewirth.[15] The idea is this:

1. Human beings are prospective purposive agents – they frame objectives before pursuing them.

2. To be such you must recognize that freedom and well-being are necessary goods – they are necessary means to *any* objective you may have.

3. An agent must claim rights to freedom and well-being, or he will be denying the conditions which are necessary to his being an agent.

4. An agent must recognize that everyone else has these rights since they all equally possess the same sufficient grounds.

From a non-moral description of (part of) human nature Gewirth argues that we must recognize rights as primitive elements of morality. There seem to be two major weaknesses in the derivation, however.

In the first place, Gewirth's 'necessary goods' resemble Rawls's 'primary goods' in that they are plainly not universal means. Although freedom and well-being will very often be useful to us, sometimes they will not. Freedom will be to my disadvantage in pursuing desired ends if I am incompetent or weak-willed, for example. And my freedom to become a drug addict will undermine my future freedom to abstain. Similarly, well-being may impede the attainment of an objective. Think of suicide or martyrdom (for example, terminal hunger-strike). If we wish to object to examples such as these we must criticize the ends involved, and this cannot be done using only the notion of agency. In general Gewirth's 'necessary goods' are only commonly useful, and to elevate them to the status Gewirth ascribes to them we must appeal to a prior system of ends (in effect a pre-existing theory of value) for which they are necessary. This, of course, undermines any claim the theory has to provide foundations for morality in rights.

Secondly, if something is a necessary good it does not follow that we have a right to it. This remains an altogether mysterious link. When I claim something to be an essential means to some end I have, I need not believe that this gives me a right to it and that others are somehow obliged to respect my claim. In this pre-moral deliberation I would more plausibly observe a free-for-all of claim and counter-claim. The notion of an entitlement is simply foreign.

In addition, the move from a mere claim (I want, I need) to a right (I *must* not be interfered with) is dubious in its rationality. While we are used to a rights structure as the most dependable guarantor of security (with our necessary goods) this clearly relies on a host of assumptions. The paradigm rights-holder is competent and secure in the exercise of power. Many real people (agents) are not. Why should they insist that the dispensation of necessary goods should be governed by a rights structure since that could be to their disadvantage? When someone has a right to freedom and well-being, he has to take them on board only if he chooses and so necessary goods become subject to the vagaries of personality. If, say, someone wanted to *improve* my share of these goods, I have the right to refuse (though my reasons, *ex hypothesi*, must be irrational if I do). On the grounds of agency alone, then, I cannot deny this paternalism as the rights thesis seeks to do – for my reasons contradict my claim to agency (being irrational). Thus the move to see claims as rights is extremely problematic, requiring a misplaced confidence in the rationality of real human agency.

Rights seem distinctly unpromising as a foundation for political philosophy. To rely on them is to rely on something totally unsatisfactory.

We must conclude, then, that Nozick's defence of libertarianism is ill-conceived. The individual rights with which the theory begins are given (and can be given) no real justification. Certainly an ingenious construct has been created on this basis, but we are left wondering, as we were with Rawls's theory, what kind of power the theory could ultimately possess. The answer, is seems, is very little.

5.

KARL MARX:
A RADICAL ALTERNATIVE?

In the previous chapters we have reached something of an impasse. Teleology seemed to collapse along with utilitarianism, its dominant species, and deontology looked badly served by both its Rawlsian and Nozickean variants. In reaching this stalemate we have run up against barriers and problems which constantly recur in the history of political philosophy: whether the good is prior to the right, whether pleasure is the ultimate value, whether human rights stymie the pursuit of the common good and so on.

Perhaps this stalemate could be resolved by a more radical approach, if there were some way of restating the problems more amenable to solution. Such is one way of conceiving the theory of Marx. Essentially this is captured in the epigram: 'The philosophers have only interpreted the world in various ways, the point is to change it.'[1] What Marx means here, I take it, is that various philosophical problems, like those mentioned above, arise because they are manifestations of contradictions or antagonisms in the way the world is – that is, in the way social life is organized. Because society is organized on the basis of conflicting interests (for Marx these are fundamentally economic and thus class interests), and because man's consciousness is a product of his material circumstances, the contradictions in society's material life will be expressed at the level of ideas as irreconcilable philosophical conflict. This conflict can only be resolved by changing the world, by instilling harmony into the basic fabric of society. This is the harmony of communism.

Of course, the commitment to communism is not merely the expression of a desire to solve philosophical problems. The trouble is that making clear what that commitment rests on is not easy. Roughly, there seem to be three views on this. First, Marxism is seen as first and last a science, a science of society and history. This science is the materialist conception of history which contends that history has a goal, or natural end (communism), and that morals or values are simply products of particular societies (they are part of its 'ideology') and hence at best irrelevant to a scientific cause. To further that cause we must change social structures (especially economic ones) on the basis of desires and interests already existing (in the working class) rather than appeal to values people may or may not have. The attempt to make people more moral, where this means believers in socialist values, is simply futile, given the forces at work in society.

A second view is that this Marxist science is by itself inadequate to the adoption of any cause and does not by itself constitute a justification for socialism as an ideal and a movement. A political philosophy is thus required to ground it. However, opinion differs over where we are to seek this ground. Some think that Marx had assumed that this task had already been accomplished – by Rousseau and the Young Hegelians. Others think that Marx was simply confused by his rejection of bourgeois morality into the belief that *no* value basis was necessary. Accordingly they seek to provide the needful in Kantianism, utilitarianism, or even Christianity. This approach is of course not sanctioned by Marx and, for reasons that will become clear, runs counter to the theory he actually espoused on these matters.

A third view of Marx's commitment to communism is more wholesome. On this view Marx was aware of the need to base deliberation over political ends on a theory of the human good (a theory of value). But because of the predominant role that social science is to play in these deliberations (Marx sometimes seems to suggest that the coming of communism is inevitable), and because the values involved are so obvious (Marx thinks that the issues are clear-cut), there is no real need to include an explicit political philosophy in the theory. We shall see better how this view holds together when we examine its component parts.

COMMUNISM AS A SOCIALIST IDEAL

The end to which history tends and for which rational political agents strive is believed by Marx to be communism. In terms of Marx's social science, communism will be a new and final mode of production, replacing capitalism (which had, in turn, replaced feudalism) – a new way of organizing the social (particularly economic) structures which determine the manner of production. It is said that the *means* of production (machines, factories, land, etc.) will be socially (collectively) owned and democratically controlled.

The details of communist life, however, are not so clearly discernible. The first and most important thing, of course, is that life is better under communism. Under capitalism poverty, degradation and 'alienation' are rife. Communism rids the world of such evils. It does so by transforming man's material circumstances and, perhaps more importantly, man's very nature. Under communism men will live in a condition of material abundance. The scarcity which forms the presupposition of all contemporary economics will be overcome. And, freed from the degrading struggle for survival, man will at last realize his true potential to live happily in harmony.

This is often called the optimistic or Utopian side of Marx's thought. Certainly at first glance it does not appear to be a very well grounded body of belief. How could there be such abundance? Is man really perfectible? Marx, however, has grounds other than wishful thinking for his beliefs.

In terms of the rationality of production (that is, both in terms of what is produced and how), communism is an improvement on capitalism. There will be no antagonism in the production process, there being no employers to strike against. There will be no anarchy in what is produced and how it is distributed – the market is replaced by planning. The contradictions of capitalism will be left behind – no inflation, no slumps, no unemployment. All mankind's productive capacity will be rationally directed to the satisfying of human want. The massive technological achievements of capitalism will be built upon so that none of us will want for anything.

Even if all this were unproblematic, the prospect of material abundance still appears too Utopian, however. Abundance is an absolute term which implies that any desire which is coherent can be satisfied. And some desires are hideously expensive to satisfy – for example, the desire to discover the scientific truths of nature through fundamental particle research or space exploration. Even if communism solves all the problems over the use of human resources, we still face the restrictions imposed by nature itself in limited raw materials. And the tendency of the human population to increase exponentially, and hence for its demands to do so too, will only aggravate the problem.

Further, it is not clear that material abundance would be altogether a good thing. For human beings, as we naturally think of them, abundance would be a kind of absolute power both over nature and, in a sense, themselves. The power to do as one pleases (to get a new car merely because the old one runs out of fuel, for example), Marx calls freedom. However, it is easy to see such power as corruptive. Without some inner discipline or sense of proportion, our tendency to self-indulgence could become self-destructive.

There must be a temptation to see Marx as meaning something less Utopian. Thus abundance is interpreted as *effective* abundance, given the desires communist man will have. The communist system will so lessen the impact of scarcity that a transformation of human nature will proceed. Once transformed, men will perceive an effective abundance because their desires will be directed to plentiful objects.

How likely this is to happen is open to question. Certainly it is easy to see Marx agreeing with it. For Marx was a romantic about human desire. With the demise of capitalism men will no longer strive to keep up with the Joneses. There will be no lust for power or for material affluence. Man will spontaneously pursue the fulfilment of his 'spiritual' nature in such things as art, sport, fellowship – but primarily in work itself. In communist society work will become 'not only a means of life, but life's prime want'.[2] With preferences like this, abundance begins to seem much more likely. However, there is still a difficulty.

It seems that the transformation of human nature requires *freedom*. And people are not free to the extent that they *have* to work to survive. (The work that is desired under communism is desired for its own sake – like a hobby.) Marx admits that this need to work will never be eliminated – technology can reduce it greatly but that is all. Accordingly there can never even be an effective abundance; there can never be total freedom; human nature can never reach its full transformed heights. And the consequence of this is dire. History's goal can never be realized. In human terms, freedom can never be realized, with the result that the social antagonisms characteristic of all pre-communist history cannot be resolved at all. It is Marx's view, expressed in the *German Ideology*, that without abundance, without freedom, all the same 'filthy antagonisms' will re-emerge after the revolution. Thus it would seem that the point of communism (it was to be 'the solution to the riddle of history') is lost. The preconditions of its being a solution are impossible.

Perhaps, though, we could settle for seeing communism as something less than a panacea. After all, it need only be an improvement on capitalism to be a rational political goal. What improvements are realistically on offer?

In the first place, communism will certainly affect the distribution of welfare. In particular the worst-off under capitalism would see a dramatic improvement in circumstances. Of course this would have to be paid for, at least in part, by transferring resources from the better-off. Even if the claims of communism to greater efficiency are well-founded, the capitalist class will lose ownership of the means of production – and the benefits that that confers. It is unlikely that a communistic share will come close to matching that level of individual welfare (we could not all be millionaires).

Second, there will, it is claimed, be an all-round improvement in the quality of life – and Marx thinks that this applies to everyone. As the social consciousness associated with capitalism is replaced, so the petty and degrading concerns of capitalist man will give way to the truly human activities centring on creative labour. The rich and poor of capitalism both move to a more fulfilling way of life. This all centres on the notion of *unalienated labour* – a process of work wherein the labourer himself initiates and controls the activity and its product. We shall examine this notion more closely later (pp. 125ff.). We may doubt, however, that a society in which the only use for labour is self-development is a society in which people would *want* to labour. Is it not more likely, as we often read in works of science fiction, that human beings would degenerate? Is it not plausible that all the activities we rate highly depend for their existence on a vitality infused by the day-to-day struggle to survive? Could we really be happy knowing ourselves to be useless (to society's and our own survival)? It is a particular religious view that God put us on earth to work and that the need to work to survive is what gives our lives their point. We need not accept this to believe that without some pressure to work men in general simply lose their way.

A third, and related, improvement which Marx proposes for communism has to do with the division of labour. Under capitalism the division of labour is carried to such extremes that the pernicious effect of any specialization becomes apparent. Specialization for the workers means repetitive, soul-destroying work (on assembly lines, for example) in a labour process which deprives the worker of a sense of control or achievement and reduces his contribution to that of an automaton – there is no need for craft or skill. Communism is supposed to remedy this degradation in that a man will develop all his potential and, being free to employ himself as he chooses, will select something worthy of his ability. It seems obvious, however, that just so long as humans *need* to labour there will be a division of labour – for that division helps *reduce* necessary labour time and hence increases freedom. And, equally clearly, the satisfaction that comes from specialization, of being an expert, is not something that would persist in a world where a man was a jack-of-all-trades. In fact it is simply not possible for someone to fulfil all his potential in all directions (unless he was very little to begin with) – for we simply do not have the time to devote to mastering more than a very few activities. Thus the demise of the division of labour is both improbable and, taken literally, undesirable. Perhaps the communist should set his sights on the much more realistic and desirable aim of making the productive process more human – promoting the aim of work-satisfaction.

Finally, in this brief examination, we should note that for Marx, communism is the solution to man's political problems. In the new classless society individual interests will be reconciled with the collective interest, simply because men will desire the common good as integral to their own. This does not require the complete transformation of human nature sometimes supposed. Men need not be saints. Enlightened self-interest based on a set of desires expressive of true humanity must itself dictate that we coordinate our activities so that there will no longer be conflict between individual and collective interests. In a sense the political process itself will become redundant because the *raison d'être* of the state disappears. In a classless society there will be no need for repression, for lies designed to fool the working class into working for the 'common good' when that in reality is the good of their social betters and merely reinforces their own chains. 'The administration of people gives way to the administration of things', and men live in a free association of producers wherein each person's good (self-realization) is dependent upon that of the rest.

Again, however, all of this seems open to the charge of wishful thinking. For it seems clear that the only way in which individual interests can be reconciled with collective interests is for those collective interests to *replace* the individual's own self-interests in his own consciousness. Otherwise there will certainly be times when one must be sacrificed to the other. Consider, for example, the issue of over-population. It is in the collective interest for people to have small families (perhaps, in some cases, to have no family at all). But it is easy to see how an individual would have an interest in producing more offspring than is collectively desirable. He or she will benefit (perhaps in old age) from the family ties – and benefit in a way the state or collective cannot duplicate. Certainly scarcity contributes to this conflict, but such conflict is immanent in social life itself. Consider the problem of congested traffic in rush hours. There is a collective interest in everyone using public transport, since this would be so much more convenient. The individual has to curtail his own behaviour to achieve a *second-best* solution – he would prefer that he should use his car and everyone else the bus.

Some think that Marx did indeed look forward to the absorption of individual concerns into a collectively dictated perception of interests. But this is doubtful. His idea seems to be that individuals will have the same sense of individuality but, rather than see conflict between man and society, they will perceive collective interests as intrinsically their own. But this, as we have seen, is a false belief. The best we can hope for is not a total resolution of this conflict but rather a correct balance between the competing claims of self and community. Marx's radical solution is too good to be true.

Similarly the idea that democracy is consistent with freedom looks odd. In a democracy the majority carries the day – their views are the ones that matter (even if they only concern what is produced, by whom and by what means). The minority is thus overruled. Their desires are not reflected in social decisions, and their freedom is therefore that much curtailed. The will of the majority is none the less coercive for being called the 'real will' of the people, the 'general will', or even a 'mandate'. The dictatorship of the proletariat is thus real (even if taken as Marx intended and not as Lenin and others interpreted it). Even in well-developed communism we cannot expect everyone to agree on policy. Judgements differ on such matters – and not just because the interests informing the judgements differ.

A final doubt is this: Can we really be satisfied with a purely technological solution to the problems of man's 'political predicament'? Marx insists there is no solution but that of material abundance. However, this suggests that we are not really the social animals Marx imagines. The need for abundance means that we can only be truly social when this imposes no costs on us.

There has never been a time when social life was costless, when some sacrifice (however small) has not been called for. How, we might ask, could a creature evolve if his essence entailed that his proper way of life was only possible after thousands of years of technological advance?

At this stage we can see that communism cannot be what Marx thought it would be. The vision is too deeply flawed, indeed incredible, to form the rational goal of a political agent. The fact that it is impossible in itself means that it cannot be the goal of history. But that does not mean that something like Marx's communism could not play this role. Assuming a coherent communist vision of the future can be developed, wherein lies its appeal? I think there are several elements necessary to a system which could plausibly be called communist.

First, it will not tolerate poverty, indeed any material or spiritual (aesthetic) deprivation, if this can be avoided. And Marx was certainly correct to say that we have the technology to avoid it (at least in so far as it is socially caused).

Second, it will seek to promote human development – where this means something less than Marx's all-round realization of an individual's potential. Crucially this development will include not just craft or professional skills but a wide education and participation in the processes that control production and political decision-making.

The third element concerns communist production – the aspect Marx held most important. Production is a matter of democratic decision. How this is worked out in detail is a very difficult question – perhaps a massive referendum to determine everyone's priorities and their intensities? At factory level of course the workers will run things – though perhaps not on a day-to-day basis (they may elect management). Clearly then, the antagonism inherent in employer/employee relations will be gone, as will the anarchy and irrationality of market-governed distribution. At what cost in terms of (some) freedoms and efficiency I leave to speculation.

The question we must turn to now is how this appeal is to be turned into a justification. Clearly some will perceive drawbacks in the communist's vision, others inviolable moral obstacles (like libertarian rights to property) standing in the way of its creation, or its maintenance. More precisely we have to ask whether Marx can offer a *distinctive* case in favour of communism. If communist claims about welfare are true, a utilitarian justi- fication could be constructed – the elimination of poverty, how- ever inconvenienced the rich were, is probably the utilitarian's priority. Similarly, if Rawls is wrong about the priority of liberty, communism could be justified in terms of the Principle of Differ- ence – if it makes the worst-off better off. Now Marx makes no appeal to such forms of justification – and if our assessment of them is correct he is wise not to do so. In the following sections I shall examine what I take to be two distinctive Marxian answers to the problems of justification.

SCIENTIFIC SOCIALISM

When Marxists claim that their socialism (or communism) is scientific they mean several related things. Most superficially they mean that their vision is not Utopian, not mere wishful thinking. It is, rather, a coherent programme for a future society and a realistic aim for us now. As we have seen, the notion of communism would have to be amended in order to sustain this claim. Ultimately, however, this realism is seen to rest not in the communist vision itself but in Marx's science of society and history. Marx claimed to have discovered the laws of social change, to have formulated a theory which reveals when change is possible (indeed necessary), how that change can be brought about, and what the outcome of that change will be. Marx believed that this theory allowed socialists to be scientific in yet another way. Because the theory claims that the working class is the engine of social change and that this class has an immediate interest in bringing that change about (an interest rooted in its present misery) all socialists have to do is reveal the *facts* to this class and the revolution will proceed. These facts centre on the *necessity* of misery under capitalism and its *impossibility* under communism. Thus socialists do not have to appeal to socialist values or people's better nature. To do so is unscientific, for it assumes that a change in people's moral consciousness (recognizing that capitalism is evil, say) can transform society – and for Marx this is illusory.

Change in consciousness can only be a *result* of social change, never a cause of it.

The science of socialism rests on the claim that man's consciousness (his ideas on morals, politics, law and art) is a product of the *ultimate* social reality that is economic (productive) activity. It is difficult to be clear in what sense this reality is ultimate. Certainly it is ultimate in an explanatory or causal role. But Marx seems to claim that it is ultimate in a *metaphysical* sense, presumably because all else is dependent upon it. The theory that Marx bases on this priority of productive activity in the course of history and in social structures can be stated thus:

> **History is, fundamentally, the growth of human productive power, and ... forms of society rise and fall according as they enable and promote, or prevent and discourage, that growth.**[3]

According to Marx there is an inexorable growth in productive power, our mastery over nature. Why this is so is not really explained – it is simply something Marx observed and treated as an axiom. The fact that it is false (there have been many stagnant economies in human history; in fact only Europe conforms, in part, to Marx's theses – I say in part because that culture stagnated in the Middle Ages) is a great difficulty, perhaps the greatest facing Marx's theory. However, granting this for the moment, the rest of the theory runs as follows:

Two things constitute the economic base of society – productive forces (machines, tools, factories and also people's technical knowledge and skills) and production relations (the relations amongst people engaged in production – for instance, master/slave, employer/employee). Productive forces grow continuously whereas production relations change seldom but radically. To begin with in any given social form, production relations will be in *harmony* with the use of the productive forces and for the most part will promote their continued development. Eventually, however, the development of the productive forces reaches a stage where existing relations of production can no longer make full use of them, indeed they become a 'fetter' on their further development. At this stage the *necessity* of continued development forces a change in the relations of production. The examples Marx gives of this are the transitions from primitive communism to slave societies to feudalism, thence to capitalism – and finally, the theory predicts, to communism. Communism is the ultimate social form and it will never fetter further development of the productive forces. How this can be known *a priori* is something of a mystery, however.

The form this takes in human terms is class struggle. Classes emerge in society as a result of ownership of the means of production (of slaves, land, factories, etc.). The class which owns these means is the ruling class and is enabled to exploit subordinate classes because it has the power to force its own terms on them. The ruling class has an interest in maintaining the prevailing class structure while the subordinate class has an interest in changing it – though this can only develop into a successful revolution when a new social structure is *possible*. And, for Marx, this is when the old structure is a fetter on the further development of the productive forces.

Socialism is realistic only when a capitalist economy is developed to the stage when capitalist economic relations are a fetter on further development of production forces. We know when this is, according to Marx, because the contending classes can no longer accommodate one another and internal contradictions reveal themselves in a terminal crisis. Marx believed that socialism was realistic (in the developed world) in his own day and that the role of the theorist was to reveal the true nature of capitalism to the workers. The revolution would then be inevitable.

The socialism of Marx is thus scientific because it predicts when socialism is possible and it selects the only possible means to its realization – the intensification of class conflict. The science is bolstered by explaining how other approaches must fail. In particular, it claims that trying to convince people to become socialists by telling them how good life will be is a waste of time – for this appeals to interests not yet born and will be overcome by the ideology entrenched in present social consciousness.

It is a common observation that Marx's predictions concerning capitalism have proved false. And it is no good Marxists falling back on the idea that these were based on a model which, though once accurate, is no longer so. It was Marx's view that reality could *not* change except as the model predicted. A science whose central predictions fail is often seen as no science at all. Certainly when predictions fail great doubt must be cast on the science's explanations of what is already the case.

Another criticism of Marx's science is of its teleological character. History, Marx thought, has a goal – and seeing a supervening purpose in history, it is generally claimed, is like seeing fairies at the bottom of the garden. Of course no Marxist could ever accept the reality of some non-material determining agency (like God or cosmic consciousness). But does this not make his teleological beliefs all the more mysterious? Perhaps not. Marx seems to have thought that 'invisible-hand' processes were at work in society. That is to say that social processes (which include human agency) combine to produce results which, while not intentional, can be presented (metaphorically) as goal-directed. Marxism is a theory about which of these processes is most important (economic ones) and what they combine to produce.

Of course this may not be a very plausible account of such processes. I think the main reason for this is that Marx wishes to begin his explanations from foundations – growth of productive power and conflict between forces and relations of production – which seem *not* to be fundamental. Certainly such processes do not seem basic; indeed they cry out for explanation, and that at a deeper level. The problem is thus compounded. Not only does history seem unpatterned (at least in terms of the pattern Marx wanted to see) but we have no theoretical base which tells us it ought to be patterned. Of course, to say that we have no theoretical base is not to say that one will not be found – though some would say that without one Marxism cannot ultimately claim to be much of a science. But if what is to be explained seems to be false, as the output of historical materialism does, then we should not hold out much hope of finding such a base.

This, however, seems an interminable debate. A more specific problem is that capitalism does not seem to be a fetter on the growth of productive power. Further, we must doubt that communism is the ultimate release Marx described. Marx argued that communism would be such a release because it resolves the contradictions of capitalism, but this ignores the possiblity of communism bringing its own distinctive fetters with it. For example, we might think that democracy and collective control may inhibit growth through the unadventurous and unimaginative rule of the majority and the dead hand of the bureaucracy. Similarly, the removal of stimulus (of need or greed) may render us degenerate, unconcerned with more power over nature. It may be, then, that communism cannot play the role Marx allocated it. And Marx's grounds for doing so are not compelling. Fundamentally he relies on an ungrounded belief in the perfectibility of human nature under communism, a belief relying more on quasi-Hegelian philosophy of mind than on anthropology.

Not only is there doubt, then, that communism is the goal of history (even in Marx's own terms), there is also a problem over what Marx identified as the means to its realization. The proletariat, the 'universal class' (united in their misery, their exclusion from power and absence of hope within capitalism) are to 'expropriate the expropriators', assume command, with a 'dictatorship of the proletariat'. This no longer looks even remotely likely. The workers have more to lose than their chains, and are rarely enamoured of the prospect of revolution. Capitalism seems to have engineered a very small market for revolution.

Scientific socialism is thus a failure. The proletariat has to be convinced of the *value* of socialism, and not merely on the basis that it is the only alternative to capitalism and that capitalism is intolerable. There are other options – most obviously the amelioration of the suffering caused by capitalism by state provision of welfare. Accordingly the communist must compete for adherents in the marketplace of ideas, just like everyone else.

THE ARGUMENT FROM ALIENATION

Since Marx provides no telling reason for us to become willing cogs in the great mechanism of history we must ask what other arguments, if any, he has in favour of socialism – never forgetting that Marx has opened our eyes to our own potential (even if he was too optimistic) and to the restraints imposed by economic structures (even though here he was too deterministic). I believe that there is a central strand in Marx's thought which attempts to portray socialism as a rational (even if not inevitable) political end. It begins from a theory of the human good and, via a series of arguments designed to show that the traditional concerns of political philosophy are irrelevant, concludes that socialism is the most rational social order (given the good for man).

Central to this approach is the claim that trying to justify socialism as fair or just or morally superior is (at best) erroneous. Such notions are 'obsolete verbal rubbish'. The idea is that the content of these notions is purely relative, the product of a particular society at a particular time. They are not and cannot be other than merely items of superstructure, beliefs which serve a class interest and whose function is to harmonize contradictions in the relations of production. Once we see what they are (ideology) we can no longer ascribe objective authority to them – they are irrelevant to any rational justification.

As a corollary, of course, any arguments against socialism based on notions of a similar kind (for example, on the inviolability of the right to acquire private property) are also rubbish. They rely on an impossible moral epistemology. Given this critique of morality, the theory of the human good has a clear field. Like the utilitarian, Marx sees the pursuit of the human good as untrammelled by irrational or superstitious beliefs. Unlike the utilitarian, Marx does not simply move from his theory of the good to the conclusion that this is to be maximized. This move is replaced by an argument like this:

In the modern world we can have social structures which are either essentially capitalist or essentially socialist. Marx presents this as an all-or-nothing choice. Either we preserve a system which sanctions private ownership and control of the means of production, exploitation of workers by capitalists, the anarchy of market distribution – all based on alienated labour – or we move beyond it. Crucial to our choice is Marx's claim that *everyone* will be better off under socialism (better off in the only way that counts – that is, in terms of Marx's theory of the good). If everyone will be better off and there are no countervailing considerations (for example, that socialism violates rights) then we must prefer socialism.

This argument circumvents moral theory. Because of the nature of the good for man and the paucity of the choice facing us, no interesting questions even arise for Marx. The (alleged) fact that socialism is better for everyone even renders (utilitarian-type) questions of trade-off irrelevant. However, there are several reasons for doubting the cogency of what is a valid argument.

First, Marx's notion of the good for man is itself problematic. Briefly, Marx believed that the essence of being human is *creative social labour*. In Aristotelian fashion he concludes from this that the good for man is a life devoted to this kind of labour. This is how we ought to live. Regardless of the merits of this *essentialist* approach, the idea that creative social labour is a *sufficient* condition of self-realization is open to question. Marx gives no real argument for treating labour thus – the idea is derived in the main from Hegel. Hegel's argument, however, has to do with the development of consciousness and hence could only show that labour is a *necessary* condition of self-realization. This, I think, is unobjectionable. We are left, though, to ponder on the relative importance of any other conditions. That there are such must be obvious. We could consider bodily and mental health, the development of cognitive faculties, of certain character traits and emotional responses, play, sex, friendship, love, art, religion . . .

If we accept that the good is more diverse than Marx supposed, then the straightforward argument for socialism must be rejected. We cannot say to the capitalist that he has nothing to lose. He may well gain in terms of unalienated labour but he will surely lose in other ways (no more fast cars, no more social status). The argument must then be supplemented – by, say, the claim that the loss to the rich is more than outweighed by the gain to the poor. But this is simply to reintroduce the problems Marx intended to avoid.

A second problem concerns Marx's dismissal of moral theory. For Marx, moral beliefs are *ideological*. This means several things. First, moral beliefs arise as elements of superstructure, in order to disguise the real nature of economic relations. We view these, not as they are (the battle lines of class war), but in a mystified form, for instance we accept such things as property 'rights'. Moral beliefs have the function of harmonizing real conflicting interests (to the advantage of the ruling class). Second, our moral beliefs are groundless – when we trace them back to so-called first principles we find nothing there. The content is *socially* generated. Marx, of course, gives this a sinister twist. It is generated by a perverse social order for its own perverse ends. The third point is that our moral beliefs are *false*. Their only possible source is a source which cannot confer truth.

The problem here is that merely to explain why we believe what we do is not to prove that we are wrong to believe it. To give another example, Marx dismisses religion as the 'opium of the people' but the fact that people believe in God for no good reason does not mean that God does not exist. At most, an explanation of belief which excludes reasons will make us suspicious of the object of belief. Returning to the case of morals, the fact that people are hoodwinked into moral beliefs does not mean that those beliefs (or some others) could not subsequently be justified.

Obviously Marx would want to deny that we could justify moral beliefs. However, it is not clear that he could do so consistently. Consider Aristotle's ethical theory. Aristotle argues that ethical behaviour is a crucial aspect of the good for man. To behave viciously not only harms others but harms the agent by perverting his own proper nature. Marx cannot deny this, given his view of life in communist society. In fact, it is a position endorsed by Engels when he says that communism will exhibit a 'truly human morality'. An ethics based on the good for man need not be a form of false consciousness, since it is based on the human sciences (which are nowadays much better informed than Marx's own philosophical anthropology).

The point, then, is this. If the above is a possible route to knowledge concerning ethics (and politics) then Marx cannot simply dismiss moral theory as a possible constraint on the justification of socialism. Such a theory may well generate obstacles to socialism (such as, for example, the necessity of private property as a means of self-realization). Marx, of course, would deny the possibility of this, since his own theory of the good requires communism. But as we have seen, that theory is inadequate. A crucial element of the argument for socialism is thus left undefended, though we can see why Marx felt no need to defend it.

A third problem facing Marx's general argument concerns the proposition that *everyone* will be better off under communism. The idea is that in the only respect that matters – truly human labour – communism caters for everyone, capitalism for no one. In fact, and as Marx admits, this is false. Although communism will provide the opportunity for unalienated labour, this freedom will necessarily be curtailed as men will never be free from the need to engage in 'labour which is determined by necessity and mundane considerations'. Further, it seems to be merely disingenuous to deny that capitalism provides the opportunity for some (relatively few) to enjoy a fulfilling way of life. The fact that they do so to others' cost simply reinforces the point that the move to communism requires a trade-off between the bliss of the few and the misery of the many. And the fact that the good is more diverse than Marx claimed merely compounds the problems. The question of redistributing (and creating *new*) benefits and burdens in society cannot be so easily avoided.

Finally, in undermining the Marxian approach, we should note that the choice between capitalism and communism is not as stark as Marx proposed. When we recognize that there are various compromises available between the two (mixed economies, market socialism, etc.) we have to admit that these various pay-off distributions have to be assessed and compared with the pure forms. We can no longer accept the simple assertion that pure communism is the only (or indeed the best) option available.

In assessing whether or not Marx's radical alternative to political philosophy is viable we have made some radical criticisms of the various elements in the theory. First, we saw that the vison of the future that is communism is neither a coherent ideal (a sound political theory) nor a particularly desirable one. Second, the idea that a science of history could justify a political theory was seen to be incoherent. Why should we accept the goals of history, as such, as our own unless some independent reason is provided for so doing? Finally, we saw that the argument from alienation failed because it took too narrow a view of the human good and too restricted a view of our social options. The problems of political philosophy cannot be solved in this way, since questions of costs and benefits and how to trade these off amongst individuals still arise.

However, it seems to me that there is an important clue here as to how a political philosophy based solely on a theory of the human good can properly proceed, without having to deal directly with the above problems. It is to the merits and elaboration of this idea that I now turn.

6.

TELEOLOGY REVISITED: THE GOOD FOR MAN AND THE GROUNDS OF POLITICAL PHILOSOPHY

In this chapter I shall attempt a sketch of a more adequate approach to political philosophy, one which I hope avoids the failures of those so far examined. It is best, therefore, to remind ourselves of the failures so far uncovered.

Utilitarianism fails because it is grounded on an inadequate theory of the good. Pleasure cannot be our sole ultimate value and if that other, more technically acceptable, maximand is invoked – preference or desire satisfaction – then we produce an even more degenerate system. A second option which we examined was to broaden the maximand so that it became a more adequate account of the good (promoting 'interests' or 'welfare'). This, however, ran head on into the problem of incommensurability of goods. The injunction to maximize these goods was seen to be no guidance at all.

The problems facing Rawls's theory of justice as fairness are equally disabling. Ultimately the liberal theory of justice is left unsupported since it relies on an unsatisfactory moral epistemology – the tyranny of the moral opinion of the majority. Clearly there is more reason than not to doubt the opinions of the many.

With Nozick we encountered a simple libertarian theory based squarely on moral rights. No explicit argument is given for these rights and there are good reasons for not treating such rights as basic to political philosophy. Again we have a theory without foundations.

The failure of Marx is similar in some respects to that of utilitarianism. The theory rests on an inadequate theory of the good (whether conceived as communism or the ultimate good of unalienated labour). Communism was seen to be inadequately worked out, if not actually fantastic, and labour too restrictive a route to self-realization. Further, the case for advancing that good, in terms of both scientific socialism and the general normative argument, was seen to ignore certain other real possibilities, possibilities which undermine the approach adopted. There is no radical alternative to political philosophy here.

Of course, this is not an exhaustive survey. However, it reveals two kinds of failure that go to the heart of political philosophy. First, there is a lack of an adequate theory of the human good. Without this any theory will simply lack relevance for, as Aristotle said, the object of the inquiry is to discover what kind of society best provides for the good of its members. The attempt to render such a theory irrelevant by relying wholly on the value of freedom (as Nozick does), or on a theory of fairness and a 'thin' theory of the good (as Rawls does) is, in the final analysis, simply to put forward one social ideal (and hence view of the good life) rather than another and thus to beg the question. The second failure is the inability to construct an adequate theory of justice and formulate principles which are to govern the distribution of the good. This failure is exhibited by both Marxism and utilitarianism.

Both elements are necessary for a political philosophy which claims to offer objective, true answers on the issue of the good or right society. Both requirements are badly served by the political philosophies examined so far. Any more adequate theory must therefore squarely face and answer two questions: First, how may we ground and develop a theory of the good? Second, how may we ground and develop a theory of justice?

ETHICAL NATURALISM AND OBJECTIVITY

Before going on to consider these questions I want to examine the view that they are unanswerable and that in any case political philosophy can proceed without answers to them. This is the view that political philosophy can be based upon some form of moral scepticism. An example of this is offered by J. L. Mackie,[1] according to whom moral judgements and values are not objective – rather, they are preferences given an objective status through error. Despite this Mackie proceeds to expound upon the nature of the good life and of the good society.

He can do this because of the general meaning of the word 'good'. To call something good, Mackie thinks, is to characterize it 'as being such as to satisfy the requirements or interests or wants of the kind in question'.[2] In ethics and politics it is to be the interests in question that hold sway, where interests are to be understood as preferences. The reason that morality and political philosophy cannot be based on something objective, like requirements or standards 'out there', is that there are no such things.

Thus the good life '. . . will be such as to satisfy the interests in question [and] will be made up largely of the effective pursuit of activities that the individual finds worthwhile'.[3] Further, 'since there will always be divergent conceptions of the good, different preferred kinds of life, a good form of society must somehow be a liberal one, it must leave open ways in which different preferences can be realized'.[4]

Mackie is trying to ground a liberal political philosophy in moral scepticism (and he is not alone in this). In virtue of an aspect of the meaning of 'good' (its indeterminacy), Mackie proposes a substantive political result. The curiosity is that Mackie himself thinks such an argument impossible:

The general meaning of 'good' does not in itself determine how the word is to be used in ethics, and neither this general meaning nor any special ethical meaning will yield answers to substantive moral questions.[5]

Much could be said on how this impossible result can appear plausible. Mackie might claim that there is nothing ethically substantive in his conclusions about the good life and the good society. For example, it is claimed that to say that this is a good life for someone is merely to say that his preferences are being satisfied. No one is foisting on him external standards or requirements. However, this cannot be said of the liberal state as the good society. A liberal state cannot allow just any preferences to be pursued. There have to be rules; rules the liberal generally bases on Mill's 'harm principle'.* If such rules prevent the pursuit of preferences (and they will, because many preferences require harm to others for their satisfaction) what can be said to justify them?

From Mackie's perspective nothing telling can be said. If my preferences include my ruling the world then a liberal state is not a good one for me. (It may be a good one for me to begin my conquest but that is another matter.) Could we say that a liberal state is good from a general or universal point of view? This could only mean that the liberal state optimizes preference satisfaction in the community (for *ex hypothesi* there is no viewpoint which matters, other than that of the individual). But how is this optimizing supposed to be what counts? Surely it only matters if we already accept a utilitarian outlook, that is if we already ascribe to a moral (objective) standard? In other words, liberalism has built into it a conception of which preferences are legitimate. It is plainly a substantive political position.

---

* 'The only purpose for which power can rightfully be exercised over any member of a civilized community, against his will, is to prevent harm to others. His own good, either physical or moral, is not a sufficient warrant.' J. S. Mill, 'On Liberty', in *Utilitarianism, Liberty and Representative Government*, Dent (Everyman), 1910, p. 73.

In general, political philosophy based upon moral scepticism will exhibit a parallel problem. No matter how values, ideals, principles and so on are constructed, chosen, agreed to or whatever, the sceptics' reality is always there to undermine the appearance of authority. We might call that reality Hobbesian. The individual's 'appetites' and 'aversions' are the final arbiters of his obligations. If he does not like something his only reason for putting up with it is that not to do so may hurt him more (in the long run, for example). The moral sceptic has nothing to say against this war of all against all – when someone makes the moral reality explicit we can have no response which is anything but superficially critical (for instance, 'Given your desires, is this action not self-defeating?').

Political philosophy needs moral objectivity. Without it we have nothing to say to those tough characters (from Alexander the Great to Stalin and beyond) who want to run society their way. Why, they may ask, should the desires of anyone else matter to them? The attempt to answer this in terms of the long run, where the unjust man cannot fool all of the people on whom he relies, is futile. Unjust men can take their secret offences with them – and being found out may not entail much cost anyway (especially in a cynical age). Further, is it not clear that Alexander and Stalin were successful?

We must turn, then, to the problem of the source of this objectivity, firstly in terms of the good and secondly in terms of the requirements of justice itself.

That political philosophy must rest on an objective theory of the good is a common enough view – especially amongst those who favour a teleological or consequentialist approach. However, there are numerous theories of the good and little or no agreement on how such a theory may be grounded. We have already considered, only to reject them, the utilitarian and Marxian theories. What I shall propose here is a naturalistic approach to the grounding of a theory of the good, an approach that derives in the main from Aristotle.

In his *Ethics*, Aristotle argued that by identifying man's nature in sufficient detail we shall discover to a fairly determinate extent the nature of man's good or well-being – or, as it is sometimes translated, 'human flourishing'. The idea is that in virtue of the kind of being man is, there are certain activities and modes of living that are characteristic of him – and we can then say that these things are suited to him or fitting. That is, they are constitutive of the good life.

The claim is that just as we can identify bodily and mental health naturalistically (via the medical sciences) so too we can identify ethical and political health (via the various sciences of man, especially anthropology). Of course, this must be a complex affair, prone to error and prematurely reached conclusions. However, this is not in itself a disqualification; it is only a warning of the difficult nature of the inquiry. The human sciences, involving as they do such imprecise techniques as introspection, hermeneutics, and the application of our own practical reasoning to evaluate the various options open to us, are not a swift route to certainty. But as Aristotle remarked, '... it is the mark of an educated man to look for precision in each class of things just so far as the nature of the subject admits'.[6]

To produce an ethics in this fashion we must determine which dispositions of character are best suited to human beings. To produce a political philosophy we must derive institutional forms from their basis in characteristic human activities and relations. For example, monogamous marriage might be based in the aptness of 'pair-bonding'. Of course there is more to marriage than this, and its other aspects would have to be given similar justification. It is informed practical reason which will produce the ideal for the individual and for society. There is no need for a mass of detail here, no need for a set of individual prospectuses, no need to follow Marx in claiming that the ideal will be 'to hunt in the morning, fish in the afternoon, rear cattle in the evening, criticize after dinner ...' For we are dealing with types of activities and relations, not their tokens; just as in a healthy diet we need only mention the proper nutrients in the proper balance and not the particular meals. I shall try to show how this may be done in more detail in the next section.

There are, however, several arguments against this approach to political philosophy which attempt to reveal it as at best misguided. Let us examine a few of the more important ones.

The first argument centres on the genuine diversity in opinion concerning the nature of the good. This diversity, it is claimed, renders impossible the project of political philosophy, since the variety of views means that there can be no coherent final outcome to the basic questions of the nature of the good society. However, despite this genuine diversity it is possible to deny that it has much theoretical importance. To claim that political philosophy must rest on an objective theory of the good is not necessarily to claim that such a theory exists or is agreed upon by everyone. We need only insist that such a theory is possible, that we have the ability to devise it. Further, there is a good case to be made for the lack of any *fundamental* diversity:

> **Proper attention to the historical and anthropological data shows that the basic forms of human good ... are recognized, by human beings, both in thought and action, with virtual universality, in all times and places.**[7]

Perhaps this is an overstatement, for there are clearly diverse views concerning some of the basic goods themselves. The religious ascetic, the jet-setting playboy (or girl), and more generally the hedonist, the worshipper of money or of power, these people can hardly be said to share a common view of the basic ingredients of the good life. But we should note that such divergence usually rests on factors exogenous to the theory of the good, that is on some religion or 'world-view', and as such can be said to depend on a theory which is either true or false. That a theory of the good must be tied up with a view of the nature of man and his relation to the rest of the universe (especially some deity) is obvious. Clearly we will agree on the former only when we agree on the latter. But that in no way obviates the possibility of an objective theory of the good. As a species our capacity for stupidity, blind faith, arrogance, self-deceit and bigotry is well-attested. This does not mean that there is no truth, only that we will often reject it on irrational grounds.

Thus, to employ a move of Aristotle, well-brought-up people will tend to agree on the nature of the good life; and it is clear even to us what that agreement will comprise, at least in large part: physical and mental health, material affluence (within limits), the development of (some of) one's potential, useful or 'meaningful' work, a set of personal relationships (friendship, love, etc.), and, to regulate these, a rational plan of life to be lived in a rationally organized society. We know (if we think about it) that these things are in fact good for us; good states and activities and good institutional forms can be derived from them. Facts about diversity cannot seriously undermine this.

However, this may not convince the relativist. For him all values are a product of a particular culture, and can only have the status of socially prevalent attitudes. That people may agree on the matter cannot alter the epistemological situation: values are not the kind of thing that can be objective. By objective is meant having a source other than personal or social caprice, a source that provides standards or requirements relevant to all people, in all times and places.

However, it is surely the case that our nature does provide such standards: it is better to have friends than not just as it is better to have arms and legs than not. Of course, it may be denied that this will get us very far. The relativist is clearly on stronger ground when he claims that complex social proprieties, such as our institution of property, are merely social products which we are taught to respect; they can have no objective justification. The idea is that any notion of characteristic activity will be too loose to yield any determinate theory of morality or political philosophy. According to Bernard Williams, '. . . there is no direct route from considerations of human nature to a unique morality and a unique moral ideal'.[8] Curiously, there is no argument offered by him in support of this view. Instead, Williams attempts to show the absurdity of one route in particular. That route is Aristotle's famous 'function' argument, according to which we can discover the function of a thing by identifying what it alone can do or what it does best. Each class of thing (or natural kind) will possess a speciality which will reveal its natural function (or end, goal or purpose) and thus its mode of flourishing. Notice, however, that this is in fact two distinct theses: first, that we can derive a conception of something's good from its proper function (its *ergon* or *telos*) and second, that that function is to be identified with reference to a thing's distinctive features.

This latter thesis is clearly untenable for the obvious reason that many of man's peculiarities are morally odious (for example, his capacity for cruelty, war, pollution and so on). In rejecting this we need not reject the essence of the naturalist approach. It may still be the case that man has a determinate function which can be used as a foundation for the theory of his good. Like Aristotle, we can believe that living things, in virtue of their natures, will have a characteristic mode of flourishing. It would, after all, be odd if trees, lions and tigers and bears could be said to have such a function but man could not. We know of these other living things that they do have characteristic behaviour forms and that these give us a notion of what it is for these things to flourish.

One commentator, however, in response to the Aristotelian question '... should we not suppose that man has an *ergon* ... ?' remarks 'The obvious answer is that one may not, unless one is prepared to say that man is an instrument designed for some use.'[9] It should be obvious, though, that to insist that something can have a function only if it is a tool whose end is designated by its maker or user is really to miss the point. We do not have to interpret 'function' in this narrow way. The real point of the *ergon* argument is surely that man has a 'species being', or essence, in virtue of which certain forms of life will be good for him, others bad. Of course, we need not accept the particular Aristotelian interpretation of that essence. It is the attempt to ground the good on a philosophical anthropology that is in question and we need not view man as a tool in order to assert that.

We have, then, an objective ground for a theory of the human good. It is our human nature. How, though, do we go about developing this into a concrete conception? There are two main routes to such knowledge: first, through the practice of the science of man (everything from psychology to anthropology). This science, as we know, is far from complete. Second, through the process of living, of trying to pursue the good in our own lives. In this process of trial and error mankind produces a body of belief of what is good, and we can take this seriously because it would be an odd creature (from the standpoint of natural selection) that was systematically deluded about his own good. Of course, men have been systematically deluded, at least in certain respects. But they have been so, not through a direct consideration of their good, but via such large questions as religion or political philosophy.

Let us agree, then, that we have objective grounds and a method of development for a theory of the human good. The final objection I wish to consider questions the relevance of such considerations. Williams, for example, argues that even if man has an identifiable function, a determinable good life, an individual does not thereby have any obligation to accept this as his destiny, for

> **... there is a genuine dimension of freedom to use or neglect the natural endowment, and to use it in one way or another; a freedom which must cut the central cord of the Aristotelian sort of enterprise.**[10]

This objection, I think, comes to this: even if this naturalism can define some form of life as good, others as bad, what does that matter to the man who chooses the bad as a preferred lifestyle? How is the good life to be an ideal for him, to gain a hold on his imagination, to be a ground of criticism (perhaps ultimately coercion) of what he chooses to value?

Of course, all moral ideals may be denied by someone or other – out of arrogance, ignorance, stupidity or perversity, for example. That there exist bad or ignorant men is not usually taken to entail the non-existence or irrelevance of the values they deny. What, then, is the point of the objection based on freedom?

It would seem that Williams is claiming that prescriptions based on such a notion of the good are not binding, not 'categorical' in the way we think that moral ideals should be. Something more is required in the way of objectivity or authority than our naturalism can provide.

But what is this something more? Man has the freedom to accept or reject any ideal. Even if a man believes in God he may knowingly choose an evil path. To reject naturalism requires not just an assertion of the freedom to choose but a rejection of the justifications it offers for a certain way of life. And this will be difficult since it seems a sound justification of a view of our good that it is based on the kind of thing we are. Our nature is not something we can deny and if it prescribes something as good for us then it can only be perverse to reject it.

Similarly, freedom is not destructive of the cogency of the naturalist position, since the good concerned will involve goals or purposes which we all normally have – those based on a concern for our own well-being or flourishing. It thus becomes irrational to choose otherwise. And this is as strong a form of bindingness as philosophers could wish for.

We may respond similarly to J. L. Mackie who rejects the naturalistic approach when he argues that to claim that

... something is objectively the right or proper goal of human life ... is [an] assertion of something that it is categorically imperative.[11]

Here Mackie intends to assimilate the naturalistic claim to objectivity to that which Kant ascribes to the moral law. For Kant the moral law is a system of 'categorical imperatives', commands which bind us no matter what we want or could want, commands which bind us simply because we are capable of rational action. Now Mackie thinks that there are no such commands, for the rationality of any imperative must be relative to some want which the agent has. But this Humean rejection of objectivity does not do justice to the Aristotelian theory of practical reason and ignores an important distinction in Kant's classification of imperatives.

The Humean theory of rationality asserts that 'reason is the slave of the passions', that the various desires which a person has are to be treated as given (they are neither rational nor irrational) and reason is simply a matter of working out how to satisfy them (efficiently).

The following example may help to bring out some of the issues involved here: consider a man who is depressed to the point of being suicidal. He sees no point in going on living, indeed has a positive desire to end his misery by ending his life. For the Humean this is all we need to know in order to say that suicide is rational for this man at this time. But say this man would thereby miss out on a future of utter happiness. Would it still be rational for him to kill himself? The Humean would say it would not only if he knew of his future happiness and had a desire to experience it. On this basis it is claimed that the only requirements which reason places on someone are those appropriately related to his wants.

It would take us too long to discuss adequately what rationality really requires. Suffice to note this: if it is rational for someone to do something that is plainly stupid, then rationality is not all that important to a theory of value. The fact that an agent may 'rationally' refuse to pursue objectively good goals merely undermines respect for rationality. For clearly it is the case that it would be better for this man not to commit suicide. There are objective standards to be applied to his action. If he commits suicide, cognizant of future happiness, then he is irrational (in a non-Humean sense), stupid or mad. When it is said that this man may not find within himself the desire to go on living even though he knows that he will be happy, it is clear that this is a pathological case of failing to see what is reasonable. Misery overwhelms the rational faculty. Can it ever be reasonable (*ceteris paribus*) for someone to ignore his own good? Can we describe it as anything other than insanity when this basic human desire is absent (as opposed to being overridden by other reasons – altruism, for example)?

The reason that we can say this, however, is not because there are categorical imperatives that men ought to observe. Mackie overstates the requirements of objectivity by way of imperatives. Rather it is because there are *assertoric* hypothetical imperatives.

In general, hypothetical imperatives correspond roughly to the Humean view of practical reason at least in so far as they can be given this general form: 'If A wills (desires) X, then he ought to do Y (efficient means to X).' These imperatives, in the Kantian schema, subdivide into two classes. First, those which operate on desires we may or may not have: if I desire to have toast for breakfast then buying bread and paying the gas bill will probably be hypothetical imperatives for me. Kant calls this class of hypothetical imperatives 'technical'. The second class are those imperatives which are 'assertoric'. They derive from what everyone of sound mind must will or desire by his very nature: his own well-being or flourishing. The existence of assertoric hypothetical imperatives is enough to ensure an operational theory of the good, a theory which can be said to be objective. Objectivity does not require that we assert of something that it is categorically imperative.

Finally in this catalogue of objections let us examine what we might call the Kantian legacy. This is the feeling that assertoric hypothetical imperatives are not enough, that the Kantian demand for categoricality is justified. As Stephen Clark remarks:

If we only value what we do because we happen to have

> **evolved that way, it may seem quite as disquieting as the discovery that we value what we do because we were brought up to do so.**[12]

This echoes the demand for the Kantian view of objectivity that wants morality written into the fabric of the universe (through 'pure' reason) rather than merely into our human nature. It is a demand, I think, that cannot be met. But this is not so disquieting as some think.

In the first place, the demands that the values derived from our nature make on us are as soundly based as they need be. Everyone has good reason to act on them. To be told that this is not enough is somewhat mystifying. Consider the parallel of basing ethics in self-interest. For centuries moral philosophers envied the support that the motive of self-interest could lend to the recommendation of an action. If only morality could be as soundly based as that. Indeed some philosophers were so impressed by self-interest that they argued that morality, if it were to have any import, must be based in self-interest. But when the good for man is shown to be as soundly based we are told that this is not enough. Yet the motive of self-interest is every bit as contingent as human nature.

Second, the well-being involved here is not mere invention or tradition; it comes from the very heart of our nature; it is the real and unavoidable representation of the good life for us. Unlike values held because of the way one is brought up, it is the real mode of good living, so that any alternative must be less valuable, less fulfilling. Of course, it must be confessed that it is contingent that our good is what it is: we could have evolved differently. However, while there is sense in wondering whether it would be better to live as some other culture does, there is no sense in wondering whether it would be better to live as horses or lions do. We are what we are. As Bernard Williams remarks,

> **If there were some title or role with which standards were necessarily connected and which, by necessity, a man could not fail to have nor dissociate himself from, then there would be some standards which a man would have to recognize as determinants of his life ... There is certainly one title ... which is necessarily inalienable and that is the title 'man' itself.**[13]

Those who look for more by way of objectivity look for the impossible and the unnecessary.

INTERNAL AND EXTERNAL CONCEPTIONS OF JUSTICE

Given an objective theory of the various benefits and burdens that life offers (though, of course, I have only argued for the possibility of such a theory), we now face the problem of social justice. We have to know how to organize society in such a way that these costs and benefits are allocated in the correct manner.

We have seen various attempts to solve this problem, most notably from Rawls and Nozick. But there are other candidates for the role of principle of justice. We are enjoined to distribute according to need, merit or desert, or to distribute equally, for example. Each candidate has its adherents, each its preferred mode of justification.

There is a common approach to the problem of justification in justice which I shall label 'externalism'· In addition to the previously specified requirements of political philosophy (a theory of the good and a theory of justice) the externalist approach specifies a relation between them: the theories of the good and of justice are to be conceived as independent. Neither alone is adequate, neither is derived from the other, each must be given independent grounds.

Immediately, then, the problems of justification are multiplied; we must provide two sources for the totality of moral knowledge. However, this dualism of justification is not something everyone would accept the need for. Utilitarians, for example, would argue that principles of distribution are to be derived from the theory of the good itself. Of course, many perceive great horrors in such a purely aggregative approach and seek to place limits on its application. They wish to supplement the theory with a principle of fairness or a conception of individual rights which will block, on specified occasions, the pursuit of maximum welfare. However, it is no use constructing such a theory without justifying the limiting conditions – and notice that there will be a tendency to do so on the very grounds previously deemed irrelevant: the promotion of human welfare. But if that is the case then utilitarianism cannot be so inadequate after all.

The attempts to find an alternative justification for principles of justice so as to make them independent are many and varied. Of the modern theories we have seen that Rawls's attempt simply peters out and Nozick's is abandoned before properly begun. The history of the subject provides similar disappointment.

Attempts to find authority in the will of God, for example, succeed only at the cost of emptying that will of any content. Since he works in mysterious ways it is not clear what his authority sanctions. Justice has not been written up in transcendental lights.

Similarly, any appeal to self-evident axioms must be rejected; what is self-evident to some is problematic, even false, to others. The real basis of belief here seems to be moral intuition: an unsatisfactory ground for moral theory. We can agree with Rawls, then, that 'There is no set of ... first principles that can be plausibly claimed to be necessary or definitive of morality and thereby especially suited to carry the burden of justification.'[14]

More promising, perhaps, is the attempt to ground principles of justice in the constraints of purely *formal* moral or practical reasoning. The idea is that there are certain constraints inherent in the very activity of such reasoning which have substantive implications for justice. For example, it is claimed that reason demands consistency, that we treat like cases alike, that we observe the principle of universalizability. However, the idea that this formal constraint (if such it be) can issue in a substantive theory of justice is simply false. It is consistent with egoism as well as altruism; in treating like cases alike I can treat them well or badly. And if formalism is consistent with (rational) amorality it can hardly be used to ground justice.

With the failure of such sources of an objective theory of justice we must face full on the problem of diversity of opinion, a diversity that ranges across the political spectrum from the anarchic to the totalitarian, from conservative to radical. That diversity lends support to the theory of relativism, the theory that there is no objectively just organization, only subjective opinions with their basis in history, culture or class.

It must be said that this diversity is more substantial and more important than that of the nature of the good. For one thing, it is not clear how it can be overcome in any philosophically reasonable way – at least, so long as we insist that justice must be given independent grounds. For those grounds seem open to attack from the sceptic. Externalism is thus problematic. In separating the grounds of principles of regulation from those of the theory of the good we open the theory of justice to serious challenge: justice may be seen as mere ideology (involving false consciousness), so that it is now a groundless prescription, something we can ignore as we please.

There are reasons, too, for thinking that these problems cannot be overcome within the externalist's frame of reference, that he is asking too much of practical knowledge. It is generally believed that justice is rational. That is to say, everyone can be brought to see the wisdom of observing the dictates of justice. Just what makes justice rational is a matter of great debate, but ultimately that rationality must involve something that matters to the person concerned (hence the popularity of attempts to explicate justice in terms of self-interest: something clearly untenable).

However, in rejecting God's will, self-evidence and formalism as the grounds of principles of justice we are rejecting the only plausible external sources for the rationality of justice. The more elaborate the attempt to construct an external source – and here we could mention contracts, quasi-contracts, states of nature, fundamental human rights and ideal observers – the more difficult it becomes to map this new 'rationality' on to the concerns of real people. The dictates of these philosophical devices simply seem queerer and queerer.

The demands of rationality mean that justice must somehow be good. But if the good is the source of its rationality then we have no need of the externalist approach. Instead we return to a teleological theory: identify the good and through practical reasoning determine how that good is to be pursued. Of course, this is the same as saying that deontology (the view that ultimate reasons can concern the rightness of an action) is irrational. But it is not to endorse a strict consequentialism. Teleological theory can make room for the notion that the good involves being a certain kind of person (perhaps a virtuous one), a person who values actions in terms other than their consequences. Some may think that this obliterates the distinction between teleology and deontology, but whatever else the epistemological point remains: ultimate justification focuses on the good and not the right. Thus to be justified justice must be derived from the good and not externally.

Utilitarianism, it will be noticed, adopts this approach. But we have rejected that theory largely on account of its inadequate theory of the good. Interestingly, when we consider a more adequate account of the good we discover yet another reason for rejecting externalism. Any adequate theory of the good will admit an irreducible diversity of good things and activities – for example, friendship, work and play. There is no common currency or final good which gives these goods their value. They are just aspects of a truly good life. Now it is the aim of ethics and political philosophy, as here conceived, to systematize these goods – in the one case into a coherent plan of life and in the other into a social and political structure. The main problem of political philosophy is thus one of systematization or architectonics.

Now it seems to me that the externalist approach cannot treat this problem properly. To abstract from concern about the good life in order to formulate principles to regulate it seems simply wrong-headed. The tendency will be for externalism to systematically ignore relevant aspects of the good in order to stress one particular aspect – be it freedom or order, even religious or mystical experience. In other words, the attempt to impose an externally derived system on the regulation of goods is likely to reveal an insensitivity to some of them. An examination of the various attempts to create such a system would, I think, confirm this – and we have seen it in both the theories of Rawls and Nozick in the different ways they stress individual freedom. Perhaps it is going too far to call this a necessary failing of externalism, though I confess that I have seen no other result. The clearest way to proceed is surely to formulate the theory of the good and derive the proper distribution using nothing but straightforward reason. This brings us to a final consideration against externalism, that of the advantage of parsimony.

In view of the problems of externalism we should be happier

if we can do without it: that is to say, if we can answer our original query about justice without resort to the externalist strategy, then so much the better. We have encountered a similar argument concerning utilitarianism: that of Peter Singer. Singer argues that utilitarianism is a minimal position, to be gone beyond only with good reason. Similarly, I am arguing that (internal) teleology is a minimal position – and it is difficult to see how it can be added to. Later I shall argue that we have no need of any additions to it. However, the present case and that of Singer differ in two crucial aspects.

In the first place, Singer's minimal position presupposes the cogency of ethical constraints (in the form of universality) in order to derive utilitarianism from a concern for 'interests'. I have preferred to follow the classical utilitarians, for whom morality must be derived from the rational pursuit of the good.

Secondly, unlike Singer, I have not assumed that egoism is a privileged starting point which requires morality in order to be superseded. The starting point is the (argued for) cogency of teleological reasoning: the claim that the only ultimate rational concerns are concerns about the good. Whose good is not yet mentioned (egoism and altruism may both be involved). The starting point contrasts not with egoism but with deontology – the irrationality of which has already been noted.

Given the propriety of the teleological mode of reasoning and the possibility of an objective theory of the human good, how then do we proceed in political philosophy? It is to this question that I now turn.

The solution that I am proposing here is to ignore the external strategy altogether and to focus instead solely on the theory of the good itself. I suggest that this theory can both ground and define a conception of how the good is to be distributed – or, as Rawls says, how best to organize the basic structure of society.

To see how this might work it is best to begin, surprisingly enough, with an example which fails: utilitarianism. This theory enjoins that we arrange the basic structure of society so as to maximize utility. This principle can be given an internal derivation, that is, a derivation internal to the theory of the good. We begin with the theory of the good (as utility), discount any external constraints (such as 'fairness') and derive the injunction to maximize as a simple entailment. To put it another way, since all we have to consider in the final analysis is the good (for the classical utilitarians other considerations, for example moral ones, derive from this), that theory by itself bids us prefer more good to less in all circumstances.

We have, however, rejected utilitarianism mainly on the grounds that the maximizing principle depends on an unacceptably reduced and homogeneous conception of the good. When we substitute a fuller and more diverse notion of the good we find that the maximization principle no longer follows; indeed it does not really make sense. But if utilitarianism fails, how do we proceed to employ the theory of the good in an internalist approach to political philosophy? It is fortunate, at this point, that we can turn for guidance to some major figures in the history of the subject – Aristotle, Hegel and Marx. Each offers an internalist, and non-utilitarian, theory.

In Aristotle's developed ethical theory we are presented with a system of virtues (dispositions of character having both instrumental and intrinsic value to their owner) whose basis is a theory of human nature. The virtues are wholly explicable in terms of the good for man (the agent concerned) and require no externalist justification. Unlike other theories of virtue Aristotle's presents virtuous behaviour as constitutive of our good, not just a means (as in varieties of ethical egoism) to desire satisfaction 'in the long run'. The whole of morality is to be given an internalist derivation.

In doing this Aristotle, in contrast to most moderns, is concerned to present justice as primarily a virtue of character rather than an overarching or independent principle of political morality. Justice is equated with ethical virtue in general, that is, 'universal justice coincides with the whole of ethical virtue and universal injustice with the whole of ethical vice'. The idea is that justice supervenes on the collected virtues. Particular forms of justice (and Aristotle identifies several) are those very virtues expressed in particular ways. The various particulars of the basic structure of society, its institutions, its forms of retribution or reparation and so on, are assessed with reference to the norms of the good society. And in Aristotle's theory the institutions which constitute the good society are generated directly from his theory of the human good (as the life of virtue), for these are the social forms which are fitted to reflect and foster the good life for man.

Notoriously, however, the institutional forms which Aristotle prescribed were racist, sexist and aristocratic. But such failings, if such they are, can be entirely explained in terms of an insufficient knowledge of man's true nature. They are failings which can be overcome within the terms of reference of the method employed. In general terms, Aristotle's inquiries did not go deep enough to question seriously the propriety of many of the institutional forms with which he lived – such as private property, female subordination and slavery. However, we can see how such practices may be better assessed in an internalist manner if we turn to the works of Hegel and Marx.

In Hegel's discussion of the relation between a master and a slave we have a critique of a particular institution along internalist lines. In essence, and in our terms, it is argued that this relation contradicts the human good, in that both parties suffer. We may, somewhat crudely, characterize the Hegelian view of the good as self-realization – a good which neither the master nor the slave can attain. Necessary to self-realization is self-expression (essentially through the process of labour), and recognition by others. The slave cannot attain self-realization because he is not recognized as a person, instead being seen as property, an embodiment of his master's will. The master is denied the good in his turn, however, since he is denied the opportunity to labour, the opportunity to define himself *vis-à-vis* the world, and because he lacks the recognition of himself as a person from the slave who cannot give this, being a mere thing. The institution of slavery, then, is inadequate to the social forms required by the good of self-realization – for all concerned. Marx builds on this to offer a similar condemnation of the relation between an employer and an employee – both are alienated from the proper mode of human labour and thus denied the only route to self-realization.

Hegel, however, goes on to develop a whole political system in this way, describing proper family life, political economy, forms of government and so on. Marx is mostly content to describe what he takes to be basic (the mode of production) and let the other social forms look after themselves. He can allow himself this luxury, of course, because of his materialist theories of history and society. This, as I have argued, is not enough. We need to follow Hegel and Aristotle to the completion of the project. However, it is important to note the caveats implicit in the theory of Marx. These concern the likelihood of false beliefs about the good and its realization. We have a tendency to be misled by superstition, socialization, self-deception, lack of imagination and so on. For example, Hegel presents his state as the final realization of the good for man in political terms. As Marx observed, however, it is still very much a child of times gone by, advocating the subordination of women, the toleration of the existence of a social 'rabble' and so on. In this respect at least the owl of Minerva does not seem to have noticed the time of day.

In general, then, it is vital that we recognize the dangers of the method employed and that we overcome the blindness so prevalent in our species in order both to recognize the good itself and the possible modes of its instantiation. In this way we may say that internalism is indeed a possible approach to the problems of political philosophy despite its having some highly implausible manifestations. The theory of the good for man is to be the fount of practical philosophy. From this may spring ethics (the theory of how a man ought to conduct himself) and politics (the theory of how society ought to be organized), though it should be clear that they are not distinct subject areas. Any normative principles which emerge will be abstractions from this reality, derivative in thought and status. Such principles are not basic to the construct nor the proper object of our inquiry; indeed they can be seen as irrelevant. One advantage of internalism in consequence is that we are not committed to some 'principle' which will once and for all, and exactly, reveal just how much weight is to be given some aspect of the good. We may once again endorse Aristotle's advice to look for precision only to the extent that the subject-matter admits.

We shall see in the next chapter just what internalism can do with the subject-matter of political philosophy. For the remainder of this chapter, however, I intend to concentrate on what seem to be the two main practical (and problematic) requirements of internalism. The first is the requirement to show that the good involved is the good that matters – that is, the proper object of concern for everyone affected. The second is the requirement of architectonics – that is, that we need to have some way of ordering or regulating the diverse range of goods that go to make up the good life for man.

PRACTICAL RATIONALITY AND ARCHITECTONICS

The first problem can be stated thus: in order that the prescriptions of political philosophy be fully justified it is necessary that they can be correctly described as good for people in general. More exactly, when political philosophy identifies something as a proper object of concern (say, justice or equality) it must be something that every individual can rationally adopt as a proper object of concern. The sacrifices sometimes demanded by social life have to be seen as somehow a good thing, to contribute to goals which everyone should have.

This is simply to restate the need for authority in political philosophy, the need for objectively binding prescriptions which are generated internally from the theory of the good. Incidentally, it should not be thought that this problem is peculiar to internalism since externalism faces the parallel problem in a particularly acute form. That is to say, externally generated conceptions of rightness or obligation have great difficulty in showing why they are to be regarded as binding. They suffer in that they lack an adequate theory of rational moral motivation – given that such principles cannot be described as simply rational or self-evidently compelling.

Of course, when political philosophy declares that something is good it is being claimed that this something is a proper object of concern for everyone. But this is just to beg the question; it must be explained how something is good in this way. Notice that this does not mean that political philosophy must justify everything in terms of the egoistic concerns of individuals. There are other views on what are our proper concerns. For this reason we can see that the present problem is not identical to that facing naturalism over the bindingness of a conception of the good life presented to free individuals. For that problem was dealt with in a way that allowed for the *impossibility* of political philosophy. It was said that our nature can be the foundation for a conception of how a person ought to live. But this is consistent with there being ethical advice (advice about how I ought to pursue the good) yet no political advice (advice about how this ought to be communally regulated). It is possible with the naturalistically based internalist method that we cannot get beyond this limited perspective to a political prescription that can claim to encompass everyone's good.

There seem to be three strategies available, consistent with the internalist method, for identifying political prescriptions with the proper concerns of all individuals. Let us look briefly at each in turn.

The first we may label 'holism', though it has also been called political idealism or organicism. On this view the individual members of society are not regarded as the true or ultimate bearers of value since the good can only correctly be predicated of the collective or state. Instead, the community is treated as an indivisible entity justified in the use of individuals for the pursuit of its welfare. Accordingly, the individual must treat collective ends as ultimate, subordinating any of his own to this higher object of concern. Thus a distinctively political philosophy can be derived internally from a theory of the good and presented as the rational concern of everyone.

However, this strategy looks distinctly unpromising. In the first place, it is not clear what it means to say that the collective as such can have interests. Aristotle observed this category error in Plato's *Republic*, arguing that it makes no sense to talk of the well-being of a community apart from the well-being of its members, since individuals are the true bearers of pleasures and pains, or benefits and harms, and these concepts can only be used of the community in a derivative or metaphorical way. Secondly, it is not clear how this 'good' could ever be shown to be a rational goal for the individual. The welfare of the collective, conceived in a supra-individual way, could never be a real object of concern to an informed individual. It could never fire our imagination or generate our loyalty save through illusion – simply because there is no such *sui generis* welfare to concern us.

Accordingly, we can leave the holistic approach to those who discern such metaphysically questionable entities. Internalism must look elsewhere for a viable strategy.

The second strategy, reductionism, will be more familiar. Essentially, this approach attempts to locate ultimate value in some aspect of individuality – for example, freedom, choice, rationality, or pleasure. I call this approach reductive because it attempts to identify some one or few aspects of life as 'the point of it all'. Utilitarianism is perhaps the clearest case.

Teleological models of reasoning require final values in the form of ends (things we value for their own sake) rather than ultimate constraints in the form of rules. There will obviously be a tendency, then, to reduce these ends as much as possible in order to simplify the reasoning process. But the end can be given an unproblematic description as the good for man – or as Aristotle called it *eudaimonia*. As we have seen, it is wrong to see this good in terms of one final or all-important good, whether that be seen as pleasure or any of the other reduced conceptions mentioned above.

The utilitarian hopes to present the end of abstract utility as a universally proper goal or object of concern. The individual is meant to extrapolate from concern about his own welfare (and any other concerns he may have) to concern for welfare as such. Perhaps he need not do so in his day-to-day decisions but certainly he has to accept this as an abstract argument if the political (or even ethical) output of utilitarianism is to have any authority over him. For otherwise he may easily endorse *egoistic* hedonism. But as we have seen, the arguments in favour of this fail.

First, pleasure (or any reduced conception) is not the sole good. Since there are other basic goods, the reductive approach is bound to leave something out. Second, even if we accept the view of the good involved, we need not accept the reduction required to make this good an abstract good. For example, if I value pleasure, I need not accept that pleasure is good as such and hence be bound by the utilitarian principle – for I need only value *my* pleasure. Third, any attempt, such as Singer's, to foist universality on to someone's concerns by saying that ethics requires it, is simply resorting to externalism (using some principle based on something other than the good) or is begging the question.

Reductionism, then, exhibits two basic failings. First, it wrongly interprets real basic goods in terms of something 'more' basic. Second, without warrant it depersonalizes the appreciation of the good so as to foist concerns on people which they need not accept. Notice, then, that it shares the defect of holism. It cannot adequately explain why the concerns it identifies as proper should be endorsed by the individuals the theory is to affect. Pleasure as such is as queer a concern as the welfare of the collective as such.

Accordingly, internalism must look elsewhere for relevance than holistic welfare and the abstracted agglomerations of reduced good. Clearly the proper strategy will be more closely linked to the concerns of individuals, that is, concerns that they can rationally endorse. I shall call this 'individualism'. Internalism and individualism combine to require that we can identify concerns that people can rationally accept as their own and that these concerns will constitute an ethics and a political philosophy. What kind of concerns must these be?

There are various theories about what the rational concerns of individuals must comprise, the theory of egoism being the most obvious. And certainly there are political philosophers who have attempted to construct their theories on this basis. However, it is certain that this approach must fail to deliver anything recognizably moral.

In the first place, a theory of justice (requiring that we give to each his 'due') cannot be founded on egoism. To be sure, enlightened self-interest can seem co-extensive with the dictates of morality a good deal of the time but there are clear cases where the egoist must go his own (and seemingly objectionable) way. Justice may require that we sacrifice some interest, yet egoism tells us not to if we can get away with it, that is, if on the whole or in the long run ignoring justice will be to our advantage. Clearly injustice sometimes pays. There have been those who have gone through life unjustly enjoying benefits more properly owing to someone else. This is merely a matter of cunning, power or luck.

Second, strict egoism bids us treat other people as mere means to our ends – as fodder. If someone has great wealth and power (and in the present state of society some do) then egoism justifies his doing everything to retain what he can in the face of demands by others. For example, he will help the poor only to the extent that this keeps them docile. And, as history shows, this strategy can be quite successful. The Hobbesian 'demonstration' of the rationality of a social contract based on rough equality is really irrelevant, since we are not in a state of nature and the rich and powerful are devoted to preventing one arising.

Political philosophy based on internalism and individualism must therefore require something like this: that we have real interests and rational concerns for the welfare of others in our community for their own sake and not merely as means to the pursuit of our own narrow concerns or private projects. Without something like this we could not convince everyone of the merits of any particular social practice, for there will always be someone with a (narrow) interest in some alternative wherein he would be better off. The man who ruled a world (and liked it) could not easily be convinced of the benefits of democracy unless he was convinced of the merits of a democratic life for himself.

Now I cannot show here that such concerns are indeed rational. But it would clearly be an odd view of humanity that denied that the fate of each member of a community is a proper object of concern to every other member. Further we can refer to the excellent case in favour of this view offered by others – most notably by Aristotle. For Aristotle, pursuit of the good life required that a man care for others. Primarily, the good life is a life of virtue and virtue requires that a man care for others and, ultimately, that he be just. But a life of virtue is only a fully good life in a good society (the fates of Socrates and Jesus confirm this), and a good society is one devoted to the good of its members. Accordingly, the fate of others matters in two ways – directly through virtue, and indirectly through our need to promote the end of the good society.

We need not go the whole way with Aristotle, of course, but the idea that the fate of our fellows is tied up with our own pursuit of the good life is surely a compelling one. It is a consequence of our social nature, a consequence affirmed by both Hegel and Marx – as we saw in the discussion of slavery and capitalism.

Incidentally, when we identify a concern for the fate of others as rational in terms of the pursuit of the good life we are not saying that every rational decision to help others is reached

via a premiss of self-concern. We are offering, rather, an appreciation of the rationality of altruism at one step removed from the
immediate concerns of action, in terms of the kind of person we
ought to be. This kind of ground is to be distinguished from
egoism in that it may sanction the ultimate self-sacrifice. That is
to say, the good for man is to be a certain kind of person, the kind
that is virtuous, and virtue is a disposition which, in the right
situation, may render self-sacrifice rational (for instance, by the
parent to save the child). A simple egoistic theory cannot cope
with this kind of rationality – the claim that in such circumstances
failure to act would render life intolerable through guilt is of
course a kind of egoistic justification, but clearly is not the real
reason involved in such a virtuous act.

To conclude, then, internalism is required because our only
source of moral knowledge is the theory of the good. Individualism is required because values (such as those provided by the
theory of the good) can only be values from a particular point of
view. Since only individuals have a point of view (there being no
general or universal point of view which can dictate to them) it is
this which must mediate between objective value and rational
subjective purpose. Accordingly, the possibility of political
philosophy rests on the possibility of individuals having rational
concerns for the fate of others to the extent that everyone can
rationally endorse particular social practices – be it capitalism,
socialism, democracy, the rule of the wise or whatever – in just
the way Aristotle, Hegel and Marx supposed.

Finally in this chapter we can turn to the other major
requirement of the method adopted which was identified earlier:
that we can rationally plan life and society on the basis of the
theory of the good.

There is a set of basic human values, each an irreducible
aspect of the good life. That is one of the lessons we learned from
the failure of utilitarianism. The question now arises, however,
of whether or not this plurality is something with which political
philosophy can cope. The view that it cannot is expressed in the
work of Sir Isaiah Berlin[15] and is affirmed more recently by
Bernard Williams.[16]

Berlin acknowledges that there are time-honoured ways in
political philosophy, where the question of how men ought to

live and organize and run their society is treated as well formed. This question has been thought to have a well-defined answer, indeed some one certain true answer. Perhaps we do not know the answer, but we can be sure that an answer is available through philosophical inquiry. We can have knowledge of the well-ordered life in the well-ordered society.

However, Berlin argues, this approach (which is the approach adopted here) faces an insurmountable problem in that human values necessarily conflict and this cannot be rationally reconciled in a plan of life or society. This cannot be done, the argument runs, because there are certain ultimate values (for example, equality and freedom, knowledge and happiness, and efficiency and creativity) the pursuit of which can only proceed on the basis of choice or commitment and not on rational principles. Here Berlin talks mysteriously of freedom as an end in itself, and Williams of a 'social or personal need', rather than a rational meshing of values. Aristotle, on the other hand, talked of the skills of practical reasoning, of ethics and of politics, in finding a rational resolution. Who is correct?

Clearly an irreducible pluralism of conflicting values leaves political philosophy in deep trouble – the kind of trouble Rawls identifies with 'intuitionism'. But has the case for it been made out?

It must be conceded that there is indeed conflict between the various pairs of ends which Berlin mentions, save in the case of knowledge and happiness, where it seems clearly *possible* to pursue both without conflict. However, it seems to me that they conflict not as values but only when detached from what gives them value and treated as ends in themselves. Of course, then, there is conflict, but why should that matter when it seems dubious that we should adopt them as ends at all? Consider the 'values' listed by Berlin: freedom, equality, efficiency and creativity. Clearly, none of these is an end in itself. We ought only to pursue each to the extent that they produce value (which is to say that they only have consequential value). Berlin's error arises from his ignoring the fact that ends have value only in virtue of a common property: the contribution they make to the human good.

This is to say, of course, that these ends are not incommensurable, that there is a common standard by which we may judge them. However, this is not some further good (like utility); it is rather the mode by which they themselves become goods. They are to be valued only to the extent that they promote the good life. Thus, for example, we should not advocate freedom in areas where people are incompetent (say, to choose which drugs to take for a particular disease), nor efficiency where this renders work degrading or dehumanizing (if it can be avoided). To say this is not, of course, to *solve* the problem of systematization, it is merely to say that Berlin has failed to show that the problem is insoluble (in principle).

> Berlin summarizes his case by arguing that because
> **... the ends of man are many, and not all of them are in principle compatible with each other, then the possibility of conflict – and of tragedy – can never wholly be eliminated from human life, either personal or social. The necessity of choosing between absolute claims is then an inescapable characteristic of the human condition. This gives its value to freedom ... as an end in itself ...** [17]

The argument seems to be that men's various ends involve a necessary incompatibility, each making absolute claims of them, so that conflict is immanent in human affairs. Further, this kind of conflict makes choice (of a non-rational kind) necessary, which is the justification of liberalism (based on freedom as an end in itself).

As we have seen, however, none of the claims which Berlin mentions is absolute. Accordingly, it is possible to deny that our (ultimate) ends involve necessary conflict. And in any case, to conclude that these justify liberalism is simply to endorse a *non sequitur*. But let us look at this in more detail, as it will help in understanding the approach adopted here.

The notion of an *absolute* claim is a difficult one. I take it, however, that such a claim is one which calls us no matter what other considerations come into the reckoning. Clearly the ends which Berlin identifies are not like this – at best they make defeasible claims. We cannot value freedom, equality, efficiency and creativity no matter what. Indeed, it is difficult to see how we can value anything in this way, save the good life itself. Even those goods we may describe as basic to the good life (irreducible aspects of it) are only good when enjoyed in the right way – at the right time and to the right extent. They can be experienced in excess or deficiency and are only good unproblematically at this 'mean'. This is why it is always best to identify these goods in non-evaluative terms. It is certainly confusing to identify such goods in a way which begs the question of their value. This is what happens if we identify them as, for example, health, happiness and justice (and to a lesser degree freedom, equality, efficiency and so on). These are terms of art, appropriated by those who wish to confer connotations of merit on something. In using them, however, we manage to say little and risk repeating Berlin's error of making a particular end always, everywhere and to any extent good. Only *eudaimonia* (well-being or flourishing) is such an end, and as we have seen this is but a name.

Let me offer a list of the basic human goods to give us something to work on. These goods are:

1. The means of subsistence; adequate food, clothing, shelter and so on.

2. Pleasure; I take it that the persistence of hedonism through the centuries has some significance. Human beings do indeed value pleasure for its own sake, so that it can be described as an irreducible aspect of the truly good life.

3. Work, rest and play; these constitute the basic activities that human beings must engage in if their lives are to be well-balanced, if they are to develop as human beings.

4. Social relationships (having, for example, friends, lovers and perhaps even rivals): these constitute the proper social context for the pursuit of the basic good activities, and reflect the fact that we have social, and not just private, needs.

Some would wish to add to this list other candidates for basic goods – for example, aesthetic experience or the practice of religion. However, I do not wish to argue that the above list is definitive, the last word – only that the list of basic human goods will be something like this. We should note two main corollaries of this way of presenting the basic human goods.

First, it is open to question (at least to some degree) just what particular tokens are the proper instances of these types. Thus, it will be a matter of some controversy as to what constitutes, say, a proper diet, a good form of work or the correct social relationships to govern this. However, it is clear that our knowledge concerning such matters is steadily increasing.

Second, each class of good is something we can have too much or too little of, that is, they admit of assessment in terms of both quality and quantity. We can starve or go to fat, be workaholics or unemployed, our social life may be too complex or too narrow.[18] The basic goods are all essential to a truly good life: that is, each must be present to some extent or other for life to be as good as it can be. The idea is that the proper enjoyment of each class of good leads to self-development, flourishing or the good life. But these, of course, are not some further good or end to which the basic goods are merely means. The good life is but the name we give to a life which successfully combines the basic goods. Metaphorically, we may see the good life as an alkahest in which the various goods are dissolved in proper equilibrium.

The charge of necessary conflict in the pursuit of life's ultimate values is therefore ungrounded. But there is a further problem in that, given the need to order the basic goods into a coherent plan of life and a coherent social order, our method requires not just that goods can be reconciled (in some way) but that a rational procedure of ordering can be devised. Further, internalism requires that this procedure be derived from the theory of the good itself. Berlin and Williams deny the possibility of such a procedure.

According to Aristotle this procedure is the process of practical reasoning, and I have hitherto only mentioned the need to discover proper extents or balances. To us, at this point, this is both obvious and unhelpful. The main lesson to draw, however, is that this is not a simple procedure nor one to be captured in a few short rules (like the principle of utility or Rawls's principles of justice). That kind of systematizing is clearly impossible. Aristotle's approach is to attempt to display practical reasoning in his substantial works on ethics and politics and I shall also attempt this in the next chapter. For now, let us note some general ways in which we may rationally proceed.

First, if a life is to be as good as can be, it must include all the basic goods. Clearly this places constraints on how we may plan and execute a scheme of life and gives us an upper limit on the extent to which each good may be pursued – for example, we may not pursue our work to the extent that it destroys our friendships. The obsessive pursuit of one good reduces the required diversity and leads therefore to an impoverished existence.

Second, the proper extent of our engagement in each basic good may be discovered through trial and error. Not only do we each have some sense of proportion (which seems all too easy to ignore), but excesses and deficiencies have a way of manifesting themselves in mental and physical ill-health. This is not always so, of course, but an individual can look beyond his own experience for guidance. The community will have built up a store of wisdom on such matters which, though often dubious, is at least something to go on. More objectively, the various human sciences can increasingly offer advice.

Third, because the pursuit of the various goods will largely involve the cooperation of others, we need to coordinate our activity. This will impose a certain structure on our pursuit of the goods. For example, if the only practicable economy is one which places work in a central position, we have to structure our pursuit of the other goods around this. Similarly, if it is good to be a certain kind of person (to be virtuous, for example) then our pursuit of the good must take into account the needs of others. In particular, we must regulate our pursuit of each good so as to foster the proper social relationships: friendships, families, decision procedures or whatever.

Finally, the need to live in a society which has definite social structures will impose a system on the pursuit of the good – it will dictate norms of family life, economic activity, creative pursuits and so on. This is a social requirement, of course, but it need not thereby be irrational. We know that our pursuit of the good life is a social matter, that it will be fostered best (and rewarded most) in a particular social structure. Thus it is rational to accept the regulation imposed by this structure on our enjoyment of the basic goods. Proper social structures, of course, are to be derived from the theory of the good itself via the various human sciences.

The last element of Berlin's theory is his attempt to mitigate the effects of his views about values on political philosophy by arguing that they somehow contribute to the justification of social liberalism. To say that a particular social and political structure is justified because there are absolute and conflicting values is to claim that a political philosophy based on the internalist method is possible without resort to systematization. However, it is not clear how. It seems curious to conclude, as Berlin does in the quote on p. 158, that freedom is an end in itself simply because there is no rational way of ordering values. Although, on this view, any particular ordering will have the status of the mere 'chosen' (in epistemological or justificatory terms), this is not to say that that ordering is best which is chosen by the individual concerned. Particular individuals are not forced to choose amongst rival orderings and it is not clear that it would be a good thing for them to do so. It may be better, for example, if they simply accept that which social tradition dictates. Thus the conclusion that freedom is an end in itself is unfounded; we could equally well conclude that freedom is a bane.

The view that liberalism can be grounded in this conflict of values is therefore wrong. Even if we are forced into non-rational, though it is hoped 'humane', choices, this is no political philosophy at all. One choice of order amongst values will be as good as another; one may prefer to put freedom first, another equality. We cannot say one is better than the other. In order to reach the conclusion that each should be free to pursue the good as he sees it we need to know that this arrangement is the best way to pursue value. But since value is heterogeneous, internally conflicting and susceptible of (infinitely?) many equally justifiable orderings, it would be odd if there were any arrangement best suited to its pursuit. How can one advocate a particular system without knowing what that system is for?

It seems reasonable to conclude, then, that systematization is both possible and necessary if political philosophy is to deliver a determinate notion of the good society.

To summarize, we now have a picture of how political philosophy is to proceed if it is to produce a well-founded theory of the well-ordered society. It was argued that an objective theory of the good for man must be the foundation of the theory. Objectivity was sought in a form of ethical naturalism. Further, because other sources of moral knowledge were seen to be problematic, it was claimed that the theory of the good itself was to be the sole and adequate source of practical philosophy. This was described as the internalist strategy which was favourably compared to its alternative, externalism. Finally, two major requirements of internalist political philosophy were identified and (it is hoped) satisfied – the requirement of justification in terms of individual rationality, and the need for a procedure for the systematization of the various diverse basic human goods.

Thus the project, in its essentials, is vindicated. I now turn, in the final chapter, to the application of this approach to substantive political and social issues. It will become clear that this is by far the hardest part.

7.

WHAT IS TO BE DONE?

When political philosophy reaches out into the world of practical affairs it does so with certain strengths and weaknesses. Our ultimate concern is with how to change society for the better, and in this political philosophy is of only limited use. Clearly with the approach adopted here we cannot treat political philosophy as a self-contained enterprise, for practical conclusions will depend upon the information and guidance provided by many other disciplines – economics, sociology, history, psychology, political science and ethics, to name only the most important. Thus where science is weak, as it is in the human sciences, our practical conclusions will be similarly weak. Perhaps, however, we can treat this as a virtue since it necessitates an open mind and encourages a proper sense of humility in the face of the obviously complex. Those who come to politics with unshakeable convictions will find no comfort here.

Hence, although political philosophy benefits from its discovery of what is and what is not a relevant consideration and its employment of a rigorous analytical approach in the search for better social structures, it must accept a clear degree of indeterminacy in its conclusions – loose ends, we might say. However, this is not to say that nothing telling can be said at all. I think we know enough to make some clear recommendations on the major political issues.

In what follows I shall attempt just this, though I do so in what may seem an unorthodox fashion. I do not seek to define some basic moral principle or principle of social justice as an ever-relevant guide to propriety. That approach I take to be misguided and, in view of the nature of internalism, hopelessly over-abstract. Ideally, internalism would proceed to flesh out the theory of the good for man until it generates a theory of good social structures. This would require theories of both ethics and politics, and much more space than is available here. Still, we must go some way towards it if we are to say anything at all about political affairs. Here I shall adopt the strategy of an issue-by-issue approach, involving only those aspects of the good which are of central relevance to the topic at hand. With this less ambitious approach I hope to invoke as few controversial claims as possible regarding what is and what is not good for man. I hope to begin with generally agreed beliefs about the good and finish with less generally accepted conclusions about the good society and practical affairs generally.

This can be done partly because of the negative implications of the internalist approach. Many conclusions about the good society could be reached straightforwardly but for the fact that irrelevant considerations are adduced to block them. The appeal to some 'obvious' principle of justice or fairness, to a theory of fundamental human rights, to the various perspectives of social contracts, states of nature or ideal observers are all popular, yet can now be seen as red herrings. Without them we can get on with the task in hand.

By way of example, consider the various political theories such as liberalism or socialism. Such theories are attempts to define the nature of the good or right society and they may be argued for on the basis of the various failed devices mentioned above (and others besides). The implications of internalism, however, are that we should evaluate such theories by identifying the theory of the good which they presuppose, assessing that and seeing whether the theory is in fact adequate to meet its own commitments. It is fairly obvious, then, that some political theories (or particular versions of them) rely on irrelevant considerations or unacceptable theories of the good.

A political theory, however, need not be treated as an all-or-nothing offer. It comprises parts which may or may not be taken together, which may have more or less value. Thus it is best (and certainly easier) not to judge them as unalterable totalities but to combine the strengths of several. Of course, the justifications of the various elements have to be compatible. We could not, for example, advocate a conservative view of punishment as retribution based on desert and a socialist view of economic equality based on the idea that desert is an empty concept (because, say, no one deserves the natural endowment and luck that determines how well they can perform).

The topics which I shall go on to discuss cover the two categories of practical thought: ends and means. We must discover something about the nature of the good society – its economy, forms of government and so on – and we must consider what means are permissible in order to create or maintain it – whether or not good ends may be pursued by violence, reverse discrimination, paternalism, repression and so on.

However, we cannot do this without some idea of the priorities to adopt amongst those ends which constitute the good society. It is to this general problem that I turn first.

A CRITERION OF POLITICAL REASONABLENESS

The purpose of the state or political community is the pursuit of the good. This good, it was seen, is the good of the individual members of the community. There is some question over whether or not a government is necessary in the pursuit of the good life (anarchists would say not) but there is, I take it, no question of whether community is necessary. Man is a social animal. But beyond this it is not obvious how the good is to be pursued for it is not clear what social structures best cater for the good life. When the basic goods in life are diverse, when each life may benefit from different combinations, when choices have to be made and priorities assigned, the injunction to pursue the good is too vague to be useful. The utilitarian problems of calculation and interpersonal comparison seem to re-emerge to block any straightforward answers.

However, I think we can derive a principle of choice which is both plausible and useful in the project of finding practical conclusions. This principle is not a principle of justice in the accepted sense, though it is an ethical guide to what we must accept as reasonable. Consider the good life for man. The good life is one which involves all the basic goods to the proper extent. A life which omits one or more of these goods is not as good as it could be. Life is less good if it lacks, say, friends, food or meaningful work. I take this to be a simple truth generally acceptable.

The good society is one which promotes such lives, at least as a prime objective. There may be other ends, other values (such as perfection) but they must come second. The question is how are we to promote the good? A reasonable demand might be this: organize society in the first instance so that each member can enjoy all the basic goods to the proper extent. There are problems with this demand – in particular some may doubt its possibility, and some may question the reasonableness of requiring some people to give up some of life's little luxuries so that others may lead the good life. We shall discuss these in due course. But first, let us be clear what our principle is saying.

If a social structure systematically denies to some the possibility of enjoying some or all of the basic goods then it is to be improved upon, if possible. An improvement would be a system which provides more people with the basic goods even at the cost of denying others inessential goods (inessential, that is, to a basically good life). We may characterize this principle or guide as a revision of the Pareto Improvement criterion of social choice. This may be stated thus: it is always reasonable to prefer that system which makes one or more better off yet makes no one worse off than its alternative. This criterion is commonly regarded as reasonable but useless[1] While it can be used to criticize certain crude forms of egalitarianism, such as one version of Rawls's Difference Principle, it cannot sanction redistribution of wealth if for any reason that should be seen as desirable – since this makes the rich worse off. Now the revision suggested here relies on making a radical distinction in the goods which are to count in a reasonable assessment of what makes anyone importantly worse off. This, of course, is a consequence of the theory of the good and the relative importance of the basic goods therein.

Our principle may be better understood through its consequences. If, for example, a system allows some to enjoy luxuries, say an automatic dishwasher, but does so at the cost of denying others basic goods, say, an adequate diet, then that system is to be condemned if an alternative is possible which provides everyone with basic goods – even if this denies luxuries to some. Similarly, if capitalism systematically denies some the opportunity to work, and work is a basic good, then we should prefer the system, if there is one, which provides everyone with work yet has no bad effects on the enjoyment of other basic goods.

I say that this guide is both plausible and useful. Let me explain how. The plausibility of the criterion depends on the reasonableness (for everyone) of a system which gives absolute priority to the provision of basic goods. The usefulness of the criterion depends on there being a certain level of material wealth – that level which allows everyone to enjoy the basic goods but which falls short of the Marxian idea of abundance. This, however, needs amplifying.

What can be said for the reasonableness of a system which gives priority to the enjoyment of basic goods even where this will have some cost in other ways? Marx said this of communism:

The old bourgeois society with its classes and conflicts of classes gives way to an association where the free development of each individual is the condition of the free development of all.[2]

The idea is that the development of any individual requires social structures that allow for the development of all individuals. This is because any coercive social relations (and Marx includes the wage relation in these) will prevent the development of both those coercing and those coerced, since both are condemned to alienated forms of labour. Hegel, as we have seen, argued in a similar way against the master/slave relation.

In the last chapter we saw that this kind of direct reliance on social relations which take into account the welfare of others is a necessary part of a viable political philosophy. Now we can see what level of reliance is required if our principle is to hold. It is that level that requires everyone to reject any social system which systematically denies anyone access to any basic good if an improvement is possible – even where that improvement will impose costs in terms of other goods to some (for example, a loss of efficiency in the economy, a loss of economic freedom or a loss of political power).

However, there are many who would see the claim that this requirement is reasonable as mere wishful thinking. Why should the rich and powerful accept it? Are they not doing rather well from a system which by its very nature denies others access to basic goods?

The rich and powerful would probably deny the Marxian claim that they suffer because of their alienation, perhaps even that excess enjoyment of any basic good (not to mention the pursuit of 'false' goods) is corruptive of the good life. Clearly they suffer much less than those who are deprived of life's basic goods, but that is not the correct comparison. The relevant suffering relates to the improved social system. Is it reasonable to maintain that a system which systematically denies some is preferable even when an improvement is possible? I shall argue in due course that it is not. First we should note how the characteristic responses to the charge that rejection of our principle is unreasonable reveal the difficulties in maintaining this position with any ethical argument.

A first response, which we need not discuss, may be to resort to 'obsolete verbal rubbish'. The phrase (Marx's) captures our assessment of those forms of justification which rely on claims that people have rights to their benefits or that their holdings are just. Such claims, we have seen, can only have derivative status within an ethical system and cannot therefore constitute any direct criticism of our criterion. They are not of the same level of generality and when made so their epistemological shortcomings are revealed.

If the argument is continued within the correct justificatory framework there are two common moves. The first is to claim that social structures do not systematically deny anyone access to the good life. The *nouveaux riches* in particular are often keen to point out that one can start out life poor but honest and work one's way to the top. Of course this is possible for a few. In theory it could be any of the poor who succeed. But clearly they cannot all do so. There have to be poor if there are rich; society needs the labour power. Equally, if one is powerful in a social context there have to be those who jump when the whip is cracked.

The second move accepts that present social structures systematically deny some (if no one in particular) access to the good life, through unemployment, poverty or whatever, but tries to justify this by claiming that no improvement is possible. This is to accept that these social structures have their faults but that any possible alternative will have more and so could not reasonably be preferred. This argument, it should be noted, concedes all that our principle requires: the unreasonableness of preferring a system which systematically denies some if an improvement is possible. The truth of the claim that no improvement is possible will be examined later.

All of this, however, may seem a little weak. And it is. For some may simply observe that their own preferences are being satisfied by this system and express indifference (or worse) at the fate of others. Thus the real case for our criterion must comprise arguments which show that the good of these privileged people requires the improvement in the welfare of others that the criterion enjoins. Remember, we are not concerned with what people want but with what it is reasonable for them to want, that is, what is good for them. The rich may want their privilege, but is it good for them?

There are two ways in which such privilege might be argued to be bad for those who possess it.

It could be argued that given the preferences which the rich man has it may be in his interests, that is those interests based on his own perception of what is good for him, to make concessions to those who are denied basic goods. Perhaps it may even be reasonable to concede to that point where he himself possesses only the basic goods – and this is all that the criterion demands.

However, this way of supporting the criterion relies on what must be a fanciful threat. If, for example, the rich man is risking revolution by maintaining his privilege he may be well-advised to make concessions. But this risk will often be negligible. And what do we say to the man whose greatest desire is to maintain his privilege (a not uncommon characteristic of the rich and powerful)? We cannot advise him to give up his privilege in order to maintain it. Perhaps he may give up some in order to retain any, but that seems an unlikely requirement. History tells us that terror and repression may work just as well (if not better) than concession and conciliation. Give them an inch and they will demand a mile . . .

In order to support our principle adequately, then, we must show that everyone has a direct interest in everyone enjoying the basic goods – an interest that reasonably outweighs any interest people have in pursuing other ends. That interest will arise because the activities and social relations which comprise the good life so define it. If, for example, the good life involves relationships of trust and friendship and precludes relationships of dominance and coercion, then we have the beginnings of an argument which will show that it is reasonable for everyone to accept our criterion.

The more familiar arguments to this effect focus on the merits of equality (of at least a rough social kind). Thinkers, from Christ to Marx, have argued that the rich as well as the poor suffer from inequality. The central idea for us is that societies characterized by inequalities (at least at that level proscribed by our criterion) are unreasonable because the activities and social relations therein are destructive of the good life for everyone concerned.

To see this, consider what one's attitude to other people must be if one rejects the reasonableness of our criterion. Can it be reasonable for anyone who makes any pretence at living the good life to prefer a system in which some are systematically denied basic goods if an alternative is available which imposes no costs in terms of basic goods on them? To say so is to insist that one's luxuries are worth more to one than another's necessities (basic goods). And remember this deprivation is not a matter of bad luck, laziness or incompetence (which might lead some to see charity or altruism as misplaced) – it is a result, *ex hypothesi*, of systematic denial by social arrangements which can be improved upon.

I conclude that this preference is unreasonable from any point of view based on the theory of the good. To support this conclusion adequately, however, we need to explain how social relations which embody it are bad for everyone. That, it seems to me, is not too difficult – for systematic deprivation is a corollary of systematic privilege and both are corruptive of the good life.

We can now turn to the second property of our criterion – its usefulness. Clearly the criterion discriminates amongst different social structures, or at least appears to. There is, however, one possible circumstance which would render it useless, that of material scarcity. The usefulness of the criterion depends on the Humean circumstances of justice.[3] Hume observed that were goods so abundant that everyone could get what they wanted, justice would simply be unnecessary. If goods were so scarce that everyone was deprived, some even of existence, then no one could take justice seriously. Only if there is a moderate scarcity, wherein everyone could be supplied with the basic goods yet very little else, would justice be a sensible criterion of behaviour. There is some doubt about whether or not Hume's circumstances are adequate. They seem to ignore the Hegelian idea of an intrinsic attachment to property as well as the relevance of positional goods (such as political authority) to just relations. However, the conditions he mentions are germane to our criterion, which does not pretend to be a universal principle of justice. It is, rather, a criterion of social choice which is reasonable given certain conditions and certain possibilities. In particular, if there is and must be a scarcity of basic goods then the advice to rank opportunities for their enjoyment above opportunities for the enjoyment of inessential goods will not get us very far. It will not tell us how to ration the basic goods themselves: whether, say, to prefer a situation in which some get all that they need and others far too little to one where everyone goes without something.

The problem of scarcity has been treated in different ways by philosophers in the internalist tradition. Let us examine some views.

In Aristotle's ideal polity the majority (slaves, women, workers) are consigned to an enabling role. That is, they are seen merely as necessary conditions for the exercise of full citizenship (and hence full participation in the good life) by others. Because of this, there is a tendency to view Aristotle as some kind of ideal utilitarian (that is, a utilitarian who takes as his maximand not pleasure but some broader, perhaps more lofty, conception of the good). Thus when faced with choosing between the complete good to be enjoyed by only a few and the alternative of sharing a lesser good more widely, Aristotle is said to have chosen the former on the grounds that this is the way to maximize the good. Because the supreme good for Aristotle is contemplation, a great deal of leisure is necessary for the good life. Clearly, the requirement to work would destroy this good and therefore to maximize this good we need to create a leisured class.

Aristotle might well have thought along such lines – but this is not how he argues for his preferred system. The reason that Aristotle gives for prescribing an élitist structure is that the roles assigned to the various classes are suited to the potential of their members. These people are thought to enjoy the good life to the extent that the limitations of their nature, and not society, allow. The lower classes are incapable of full citizenship. Now Aristotle may have been wrong in believing this, but clearly the approach adopted avoids the need to resort to choosing between the alternatives which scarcity supposedly forces on us.

This same happy result was achieved by Marx, though instead of a neat class structure he relied upon the elimination of scarcity by technological progress. No want, he argues, need go unsatisfied. This is the precondition of human self-realization.

Clearly both of these answers to the problem posed by scarcity are incredible. We need not be egalitarians to dismiss Aristotle's natural aristocracy and the impossibility of the Marxian solution has already been shown. Similarly, Hegel's response is less than convincing. Hegel allows that some may be used as fodder to maintain the rational capitalist economy. Such economies, Hegel observed, will generate an unemployed and eventually socially excluded 'rabble'. This is justified, however, in terms of a holistic conception of the good – the sweep of 'reason' through human history.

Although these treatments of scarcity are inadequate by themselves, they do suggest that the problem is not intractable. For when we concentrate on basic human goods we may be surprised to learn that scarcity is not an unavoidable fact of life. Except where shortages are caused by natural disaster and human incompetence or contrivance, human societies in most times and places have had the capacity to provide these goods. Consider the list offered in the last chapter: the means of subsistence, pleasure, work, play and social relations. Even when we add other plausible candidates such as the ability to reason clearly or aesthetic experience, there seem to be no basic goods which are prohibitively expensive – at least in theory. It would seem, therefore, to be a failure in human planning or imagination, or more likely the adoption of alternative (and hence inferior) ends which creates this scarcity. In fact, most advocates of a particular system of production and distribution (whether they be socialists or libertarians) claim that their system will deliver the goods if it is allowed to work properly.

There is, however, one source of scarcity which makes it difficult to meet even these limited demands – over-population. A problem of utilitarian theory is the claim, which utilitarianism involves, that a universe containing two million happy sentient beings is better than one which contains only half that – solely in virtue of the numbers involved. There is here a commitment to population increase so long as this involves a pro rata increase in utility. And this seems perfectly reasonable, given the utilitarian view of the good. The real problem arises if, as seems possible, an increase in numbers will increase total utility yet lower the average. In other words the lowering of the quality of life can come to seem rational on utilitarian grounds.

This problem may not appear to trouble us, since our basic concern is the good life and this cannot be sacrificed for the sake of some reduced conception of the good. However, a similar problem arises if it is suggested, as it often is, that life itself is a basic good. The demand to create and maintain life (as an end in itself) becomes a fundamental drain on our resources and will ultimately create the scarcity which undermines our criterion's usefulness.

The answer to this problem is the obvious one: life itself is not to be considered a basic value; death, and non-existence, by the same token, are not themselves basically bad. There are two major arguments against this view of the value of life. The first we may call naturalist or humanist, the second theological.

Before examining them, however, let us be clear what is being objected to. Life, I am saying, is valuable only as a means to the enjoyment of intrinsic goods. There are several such goods, as we have seen. They are the things which make life worthwhile or fulfilling. Life, however, is not one of them. Rather, it is to be seen as the necessary precondition for experiencing the delights (or otherwise) that the world offers. Essentially, this is because it is not true of life that we should always choose it (it is not always worth living), whereas this is true of the basic human goods in general.

Perhaps a parallel with utilitarianism will be helpful. For utilitarianism, the sole good as an end is pleasure, where this means the experiencing of pleasure (for, of course, pleasure only exists as an experience). Clearly it would be absurd to then claim that experience itself is good in itself, since experiences may be truly awful. The claim that life is itself a basic good seems to me to be similarly wrong.

The naturalistic argument in favour of life's being valuable in itself is said to derive from Aristotle, who is interpreted as holding that the general desire for something is a sufficient condition of that thing's being valuable. This is converted into 'valuable in itself' by Finnis,[4] who argues that life itself is a basic good 'corresponding to the drive for self-preservation'. Life is a value in itself, it seems, because everyone desires it for its own sake.

However, this is not quite how the argument goes. On closer examination we see Finnis to be redefining his term. By 'life' he means not just being alive but 'every aspect of the vitality which puts a human being in good shape ... which includes bodily health ...'[5] Now of course health and vitality are basic goods (though these will be question-begging labels for any particular activity or state without the relevant demonstration that they are healthy or vital). They correspond, incidentally, in the main, to the basic good I have called 'means of subsistence'. This, by the same token, however, is not a case for saying that life itself is a basic good.

Similarly, in the relevant passage from Aristotle, the concern is with how life is good and pleasant for the virtuous man and with how he is to value the life of his friends. Aristotle actually says that 'we must not apply this to a wicked and corrupt life nor to a life spent in pain'.[6] Life has the value it has in virtue of how good it is.

Clearly, then, life as such has not been shown to be a basic good. And to label that which is such a good (health or vitality) 'life' is to confuse an important issue. We must be able to say that life is valuable, that it is reasonable to choose it, only in certain conditions. Indeed, this seems essential to a naturalistic theory of the good. Man's good is not life but the good life. The life of a human vegetable is not desirable in any way, even if the alternative is death. Such a state is something we rightly dread and may reasonably assess as a valueless life.

The second class of argument in favour of the intrinsic value of life is the theological one. The central idea seems to be that God has invested (human) life with some purpose, a purpose which we cannot fully comprehend, and that the only occasion on which we may say that a life has no value is when that life is over. That is, we may never say of an ongoing life that it has no value.

I find this argument, if it really is an argument, totally elusive. As a philosophical position it is open to serious challenge. First, to rely on the existence of God is to rely on something that falls short of anything like rational certainty. This simply multiplies the sources of doubt. Second, even if God does exist it is not obvious that he has invested life with any purpose or, if he has, what that purpose is. Third, it is not clear why *we* should adopt that purpose (assuming we could discover what it is) as our own, especially when it will often run counter to our otherwise reasonable choices (regarding procreation in particular). The fact that God values life does not make it reasonable for me to value it, especially as a good in itself. To say so violates the constraints of individualism outlined in the last chapter.

We have, then, a case for claiming that scarcity is not the problem it seems, at least if we restrict ourselves to a concern with the basic human goods. The criterion on offer has thus been defended as plausible (in terms of its ethical presuppositions) and useful (in that the conditions for its application seem to obtain).

Let us now turn to the major areas of application of the criterion in order to assess the relative merits of the rival political theories.

POLITICAL ECONOMY

Many people would agree that the single most important set of processes in society is its political economy. It clearly is the most important system with reference to determining the individual's enjoyment of basic goods, for it is this system of institutions and practices in which the labour of human beings combines with the various other means of production to produce, distribute and exchange those goods and services deemed valuable.

The institutions and practices concerned are those which govern ownership (of labour power and other means of production) and which define the various legal freedoms and powers which owners may exercise. In turn these will determine the kind of social relations which govern the economic processes. These institutions and practices constitute the kind of economy we have; most obviously we may have a capitalist economy (characterized by private ownership of the means of production, free markets and the employer/employee relation) or a socialist economy (characterized, if only in theory, by social ownership of the means of production, collective planning and the free association of producers). There may, of course, be other types of economy; most real-world economies, for example, fall somewhere between these two 'pure' types.

The first thing to note about assessing rival economic systems is that our ultimate concern should not be over what is deemed valuable (what people actually want) but with what is in fact valuable (what people must reasonably want). The two will diverge where people have irrational or perverted preferences – the many causes of which we need not list. We saw in our discussion of preference utilitarianism why this 'liberal' economic outlook is to be rejected.

The second point to note is how our criterion is to be applied in this assessment. If an economic structure systematically denies some people the possibility of enjoying some or all of the basic goods then it is to be improved upon, if possible. We are to prefer the system, if there is one, which provides more people with the basic goods, no matter what the costs in terms of other goods.

The importance of the economy lies in its impact on the enjoyment of the basic goods of life. It is difficult to enjoy any good if one is denied the means of subsistence. Nevertheless, I propose here to discuss political economy in the context of the provision of just four basic goods. These are first, the means of subsistence; second, the provision of work; third, the quality of work; and fourth, the social relations governing the work process.

With regard to these goods there are three questions that seem relevant here. First, can the system produce enough of the means of subsistence (at least) to meet the reasonable demands of all the members of society? Essentially, in view of our remarks about scarcity, this is a matter of the rationality and efficiency of the system. Is the system directed towards the provision of basic goods (at least giving them priority) and does it do so in a way that is not wasteful of resources (where this is judged by comparing it with rival systems)?

Second, are the processes involved in the system (processes of production, distribution and exchange) and the social relations governing them, of the proper kind? That is, are they basically good?

Third, if the system falls short in some way, say by condemning some to soul-destroying poverty or labour, is an improvement, in the terms of our criterion, possible?

Let us begin our discussion of these issues in the context of a capitalist economy.

With reference to our first question, capitalism clearly has few problems with its productive capacity. Even Marx was impressed with this feature of the capitalist system. However, capitalism faces severe problems concerning its rationality and efficiency. This is to say that although the system has the productive power to meet reasonable material needs it does not do so at all for some people and does so inefficiently for others.

In the open market only those goods are produced for which an effective demand exists or can be created. Those who cannot pay cannot consume. Production and allocation are functions of effective consumer demand so that it is clear that markets operate with no objective criteria of value – they rest on individual preferences. This means that basic goods as such are not given their due importance. The needs of the poor will be ignored and the rich will be free to pursue their own goals, however degenerate. And that capitalism will produce these two classes of people seems inevitable. Of course, there are those who think that an unfettered capitalist economy will be self-regulating (guided, as they say, by an 'invisible hand') and thereby ensure that every member of society will enjoy prosperity and freedom. But few of us can accept such wishful thinking in view of what history tells us. Even those who advocate capitalism tend to accept that extreme inequality of wealth is not accidental to the system (that it is not the fault of meddling governments, or whatever) but is justified none the less. It is clear that the freedoms and motivations characteristic of capitalism result in extreme concentrations of wealth. With few exceptions the rich get richer and the poor remain. Further, no capitalist system seems immune to the cyclical process of boom and slump, of rapid growth and recession with its concomitant unemployment.

Again, capitalism seems unable to provide what are called 'public goods', that is, goods which when provided may be enjoyed by everyone regardless of whether or not they pay for them. Defence, law and order, and infrastructure (roads, sewers, etc.) are often listed amongst such goods. Everyone has a reason to 'free ride', relying on others to provide the good. The free market, characterized by non-cooperative motives, does not provide such goods, or does so unsatisfactorily, since the demand for them is not one any individual may care to make effective.

More controversially, it may be argued that the capitalist system is a singularly inefficient way of providing goods which everyone must have. To provide such goods as health care and education privately not only means that only those who pay are catered for (so that these basic goods are denied to some) but that more resources are consumed than would be required in an equivalent public provision of such goods. There is a case to be made, and it is essentially the socialist case, for the provision of such goods publicly on the grounds of efficiency. By eliminating profit, enjoying massive economies of scale (in a national provision) and by cutting out duplication, advertising, 'unnecessary' options (such as some cosmetic surgery), we can enjoy the same services more cheaply, that is, spend less of our total resources on them.

Now much of this will be contested on technical grounds by the defenders of capitalism. They will point out how competition keeps everyone on their toes, how bureaucrats cause more waste than other savings can possibly compensate for, and how public provision tends to give people what suits the providers rather than what people actually need. Of course there will be some truth in this. Whether there is enough truth is doubtful, and whether the failings of socialism are inevitable is equally so.

However, it is not the task of political philosophy to decide such matters. They must be left to that 'dismal science' of economics, and to the observations of us all of what happens in practice. Whatever the answers, though, it is clear that capitalism is not rational and efficient. The distribution of goods will be such that some will be systematically denied the necessary level of basic goods. We must therefore seek to improve upon this system if possible.

Turning to the second question, it seems to me clear that both the social relations of production and the work processes involved in capitalism are bad.

Not only do capitalist economies give rise to massive inequalities of wealth and power (to the extent that the rich come to have only economic ties with the poor so that there is no sense of community), but the very work relation itself (that of employer and employee) is perverse. I know of no reasonable argument in favour of this relation. At best it may be regarded as a necessary evil, as a necessary part of a system which is productive of the greatest good. However, even this is contested by liberal utilitarians such as J. S. Mill.

> **To work at the bidding and for the profit of another without any interest in the work ... is not, even when wages are**

> **high, a satisfactory state to human beings of educated intelligence, who have ceased to think themselves as naturally inferior to those whom they serve.**[7]

One does not need to be a Marxist, then, to recognize that this social relation is in itself bad, making a basic antagonism of interests inevitable in the productive process. More telling, in an ethics and political philosophy which places at its heart the human good one description of which is self-realization, how could one possibly tolerate a system which consigns the majority to this kind of subservience in one of life's primary activities if an improvement is possible?

Similarly, it is clear that capitalism forces the adoption of dehumanizing and degrading work processes in its search for profit in the face of relentless competition. Assembly-line production is but one example of the excessive division of labour.

Now the proponent of capitalism may challenge this in two ways. Though he cannot dispute the facts about the drawbacks of capitalism, he may deny that work is a basic good (and hence that our criterion can be applied on its behalf). And second, he may deny that an acceptable improvement is possible.

Why then do I claim that work is a basic good? To understand this we must see that work is to be conceived broadly as productive activity, both in transforming nature to suit our purposes and in the production of ideas and theories. Thus, for example, the production of theories of ethics and political philosophy (or the exercise of practical reason) is a form of work.

Some form of this activity, I claim, is a basic human good. Not just any work activity is good, of course, since this activity, like any other, can be perverted. A life without proper work could never be considered the good life for man, for such a life would be missing something vital. There are two classes of argument aimed at this conclusion. The first relies on empirical data about the quality of a life deprived of proper work activity. The second relies on the claim that human nature is such that work activity is essential to self-realization.

Philosophers like Hegel, Mill and Marx agree that a genuinely fulfilling life is one which demands the use of one's faculties and talents, for in this one enjoys a peculiar, and superior, satisfaction. The satisfaction from achievement here is preferable to the merely passive pleasure enjoyed, say, by the drug user. The essentialist arguments generally begin by noting what makes us human: man as a language-user, a tool-user, a planner as well as a doer. From this it is concluded that the activities of learning, reasoning and labouring are essential to our development as human beings. Both types of argument seem to me to contain much truth, indeed they are interdependent. We derive satisfaction from wholesome work not by accident but because of the kind of creature we are.

Now capitalism not only perverts the activity generally, it denies to some the opportunity to work at all. Consider an unemployed craftsman who owns no means of production besides his own labour power. This man is denied the opportunity to exercise his talent, to gain fulfilment; it is not possible that he can labour even as a hobby since he has no resources available on which to labour. This state of affairs is therefore, again, to be improved upon if possible.

What, then, of the claim that no improvement is possible? It is simply false. In the real world we have instances of economies which are improvements on capitalism in the sense I mean. Consider the case of 'welfare' capitalism. This system moves towards the resolution of the problem of lack of means of subsistence for some by providing social security. There must be some doubt over whether it can solve this problem completely, however, since in a basically capitalist system this provision will always be under pressure and thus be insecure, especially when unemployment is high – always assuming that welfare provision is set at an adequate level to begin with.

However, this system by itself cannot provide the basic good of work to everyone, still less ensure that that work is of a proper kind. Can we make further improvements? There are two established routes to providing everyone (or nearly everyone) with work: the partial economic management inspired by Keynes and the total economic management inspired by Marx. Both of these are improvements in a narrow sense (that is, purely in terms of the basic good of work) but we may now be getting uneasy about their costs in terms of other goods. That aside, however, we should note that neither offers any improvement in either the work process itself (both systems mimic capitalism) or in the social relation governing work (Eastern Bloc socialism merely replaces the private employer with the state).

Is there, then, something else? I think so. We have to devise a system which regulates the economy in such a way as to provide everyone with the opportunity to work. This requires regulation by the public authority. Further our economy must not comprise employers and employees, since production must be carried on by independent or freely associated (that is, cooperatives or partnerships) producers. Again, what is produced and how must be subject to regulation. The economy must not waste resources in the production of the junk characteristic of so much capitalist enterprise nor can it allow inappropriate work processes. Thus the public authority must act as a product and process licensing board.

This system may be called 'market socialism'. For within the constraints mentioned above there will be a market in goods and competition in their provision. However, not all goods will be produced and allocated in this way since, as we have noted, there are services which may be more efficiently provided publicly (for example, health and education).

There are two forms of criticism which we need take seriously here. The first relates to the possible inefficiency of our system. However, only if inefficiency were so bad that it created a scarcity of basic goods would our criterion fail to sanction it. This, I think, is unlikely. The second relates to the consequences of adopting this system with regard to our enjoyment of other goods, especially freedoms. By and large, however, the same freedoms may be enjoyed under this system as under any civilized regime except for the freedoms to acquire great wealth or to employ other people. The state need not control everything; indeed it is better that it should not for, as liberals often point out, a bureaucrat will be more concerned with his own good than the good of those he plans for. When it is said that denying economic freedoms quickly modulates into a generalized totalitarianism, it is not the economy which does this but the people controlling it. Accordingly we must turn to an examination of government in order to assess this danger.

THE NATURE OF GOVERNMENT

The nature of government is a function of its form and its extent. By form I mean that aspect of government to do with who rules, that is, who formulates and enacts policy. Traditionally these forms are given names such as autocracy, aristocracy or democracy. Systems in the real world are more complex affairs, of course. By extent I mean that aspect of government to do with what is ruled, that is, what classes of people and activities fall under governmental control. Here we employ the range of labels between anarchy and totalitarianism.

The nature of government is to be justified in terms of its proper function, which we can identify as the pursuit of that aspect of the good which government alone can pursue or that which it can pursue best. The proper function of government is therefore a largely empirical problem. We have to identify those aspects of the good best suited to government provision or control, and identify the form of government best able to perform this function.

Those aspects of the good society best suited to government control are a matter of serious dispute. There can be no presumption in favour of any extreme (total freedom or total control) so each proposal has to be assessed on its merits. For the sake of discussion, however, and because of a general suspicion about the value of control, I shall begin at the anarchist end of the spectrum and inquire which of its failings can be remedied by government.

Anarchy may have its attractions for the romantic amongst us but it is clear where its weaknesses lie. Can we really believe that the provision of important goods, many of them public goods, is possible through the free cooperation of those concerned? Consider, for example, the provision of defence, the maintenance of law and order, the regulation of the economy and the protection of the environment. Is it not clear that we need some public authority to provide these goods? Again, is it not preferable that those goods which may be better provided publicly, such as health and education, be controlled by such an authority? Another example may be the funding of research into pure science.

Such a conception of the proper business of government

approximates to that prevalent in modern Western nation states (though the regulation of the economy is more pervasive). What, though, of the value of greater control, where governments invade the much more personal aspects of our lives?

The liberal philosopher, J. S. Mill, argued strongly that such personal control is only justified to prevent a person harming others, since a person's own good is best left to himself. This notion, which carries great intuitive appeal, is generally called 'the harm principle'. However, it is clear, even to Mill, that this principle is not axiomatic. It has to be derived from some notion of what is good (for Mill this was utility) and is therefore unlikely to be exceptionless. It is therefore best to treat it as a starting point, like anarchy, and ask what failings it has that can be remedied by government.

Mill's harm principle is intended to block paternalism (coercing someone to do what is for his own good). The central problem in stating the principle is that defining 'harm' with the required accuracy is near impossible (what is to count as harm?). For our purposes, however, we need only note that Mill's case for his principle, relying ultimately on its utility, is weak. It relies on the gross generalization that the individual is the best assessor and pursuer of his own good or, if he is not, that the costs or ineffectiveness of outside control render paternalism self-defeating. This is simply untrue. Examples such as the compulsory use of seat-belts in cars and crash-helmets on motorcycles show both that individuals left to themselves are often incompetent and careless, and that paternalism can be effective.

In principle, then, there is a case for saying that, other things being equal, government is justified in forcing people to pursue what is good for them in any area of life. However, it is clear that such a course of action would be disastrous. In the first place, government is not so trustworthy. The ends of politicians and bureaucrats more faithfully reflect their own perceived good than the general good. Second, no human institution could sensibly and efficiently deal with the totality of human affairs. Third, it is clear that the good life for man is one of developed faculties and responsible outlook, and that self-realization involves the power to choose and act wisely. To this end people must be allowed to make mistakes and to make those mistakes in areas of some significance for the quality of their lives. We learn by trial and error. Choosing friends, mates, occupations, hobbies and so on seem to be clear cases. Further, human arrogance, amongst other things, will make coercion self-defeating.

This will mean that those large areas of political, personal and intellectual freedoms which many hold so dear are best left excluded from the remit of government. The exercise of such freedoms is essential to the good life for man. Society, to use Popper's term, is best if characterized by this degree of 'openness',[8] that is, where people are free to conjecture and criticize, and where the public authority takes heed of such criticism. In other words, free speech and inquiry and free media do much more good than harm.

Given this proper extent of government, what form should that government take? It would seem that no particular structure can be guaranteed to concern itself with its proper function. Theoretically the options fall between two significant poles – the rule of the people (democracy) and the rule of the wise (or good). In the modern world there is a tendency to assume that good government is democratic and to call whatever one thinks good 'democratic'. But while the term is vague, it is not that vague. Similarly, whatever system is preferred will tend to be thought of as the rule of the wise. For democrats, wisdom is possessed by the people. Lincoln, for example, opined that you cannot fool all of the people all of the time. This may be so, but to distinguish between democracy and the rule of the wise one need only note that in a democracy you need only fool enough of the people enough of the time (to get elected or re-elected, or to get some particular policy through).

What, then, are the real merits of democracy – and by 'democracy' I mean here those political forms characteristic of Western Europe? First, there is the fact that such systems, more than others, tend to concern themselves in the proper spheres and to do so with at least some competence. The public authority has to be responsible, at set intervals, to the public and this facilitates revision of bad policy and the replacement of incompetent and corrupt officials. Further, such systems allow open political participation and this 'supreme' practical activity is, as Mill observed, an essential aspect of the self-development of man as a progressive being. A person without politics is importantly ignorant and to that extent inferior or underdeveloped.

But, as hinted at above, democracy is not ideal. The rule of the majority may be tyrannical or repressive (where some minority can be identified – this is commonly a matter of race, religion, even language); unimaginative and naturally conservative; susceptible to simplistic policy options; perhaps degenerate in its conception of the human good. Clearly these evils do manifest themselves in our democracies. Since no radical alternative is available which is even tolerable we must content ourselves with some tinkering with the system.

We can identify several constraints which help to counteract these unpleasant tendencies. The process of representation may be seen as a process of filtering out the more practically wise amongst us. It is not anywhere near successful, of course, but it seems to avoid the worst excesses which a direct system would manifest. A second constraint is a bill of rights. Given an independent judiciary, such a bill will help protect various minority groups from overt persecution by defining liberties and opportunities which require more than a simple majority to abolish. Of course such liberties will not include those which make transition to a more reasonable social system more difficult (for example, the right to hire labour power). A third constraint is a second, revising chamber in the legislative process. This, it is hoped, will help filter out bad policy. To avoid democratic whim it will, of course, be non-elected. Instead of a chamber composed (ridiculously) of hereditary aristocrats and those selected by executive patronage we would do better with a selection of those who have demonstrated practical wisdom – from industry, science and the arts. The mechanism of selection may vary – perhaps certain posts would simply carry the responsibility of membership. Finally, we can stress the need for open government. Government which proceeds by secrecy and deceit cannot possibly be justified. It loses its democratic merit (even if people consent to it) and only through arrogance could it be called wise.

Now all of this is intended to provide a framework wherein each individual can pursue, and will be encouraged and helped to pursue, the good life for man. To this end it is designed to protect certain freedoms (personal, political and intellectual), which defenders of capitalism insist require a free economy (and all that this entails). This connection of freedoms is spurious, however. Clearly capitalism can and does exist with repressive regimes. The threat to valuable freedoms is real, of course – and will always be so. At what point the loss of some freedoms (say economic ones) necessitates the loss of all others it seems impossible (and foolish) to say. Some governments which control the economy control nearly everything else. But there are governments which control everything but the economy.

To repeat, no system guarantees good outcomes. Any system could ignore our criterion of social reasonableness, given earlier. The good is more importantly served by the people who participate in the policy-making process – and in our democracy this will be nearly everyone. Thus the most important contribution to the goodness of society comes from education: the skills, knowledge and virtue of a people are the real factors in determining whether government works well.

WAYS AND MEANS

We have, then, some idea of what the good society would be like. And we have some reason to believe that a democratic, open society is a good means to it (as well as part of it). But there are other problems to consider and it should be clear that our criterion is of no real help. For that only tells us what is reasonable. What are we to do when people are (or were) unreasonable? For example, what are we to do when the state is repressive and stands in the way of progress towards the good society; or when individuals act so badly that they go beyond the bounds of 'acceptability'; or when someone or some group has been so badly treated that merely to give them the basic goods may seem inadequate? It is to instances of such problems that we must now turn.

Political Violence

When people resort to violence for political ends they are thought either heroes or villains. It is an extreme activity involving extremes of courage or extremes of depravity, carried out by freedom fighters or terrorists. Is it, then, that the justification of a particular act of violence depends in which side one supports? I think not, for, as I shall argue, there are proper interests and proper ways of pursuing them.

Much debate about violence and the threat of violence concerns its definition. There are two schools of thought on the matter. On the one hand there are those who try to capture a definition which 'stands in some tolerable relation to ordinary usage and belief'.[9] And on the other there is the attempt, associated with radical thought, to widen the scope of the concept to include much more of what it disapproves of, for example, 'exploitation', the toleration by the rich of poverty and, generally, those activities which our criterion deems unreasonable.

We can gain little by entering into this controversy. Suffice it to say that it is not only criminals who use violence or terror. The state uses violence to apprehend and imprison those who offend against its laws and employs terror (in the threat of the use of nuclear weapons, for example) to deter potential aggressors. Similarly the use of violence and terror is not the only (or even the worst) source of evil in the world (that is, if we define it to mean other than 'cause of great evil'). For the people of a rich nation to ignore preventible and massive suffering in other nations is perhaps the greatest evil in the world today. It matters little, save to rhetoricians, what such practices are called. As we shall see, simply to label something an act of violence or terror is not by itself a condemnation. Nor is to deny that something is an act of violence in itself a way of removing some or all due disapprobation. It is a consequence of our teleological approach that we cannot judge an act simply on the basis of its coming under some general description, like 'act of violence'. Of course some descriptions do carry such implications (for example, 'wrong') but then the judgement has already been made.

The problem of violence is a version of the more general problem of the use of unsavoury means to attain desired ends. Other cases include deceit, concealment, punishment and repression. Do the ends justify the means?

In the first place we should note that nothing else can: means can only be justified by their ends. A justified end is a necessary condition of justifying the means to it. This is a simple consequence of the teleological approach. The real issue is whether or not any ends are sufficiently important to sanction odious means. Are these evils necessary?

To restrict ourselves here to the use of violence and terror, consider the views of those who would maintain an absolutist position against it. Pacifism as a deontological view, however, is irrational (like all deontological views) and as a teleological view is naïve. The deontological view is to be rejected because an act can have no value (goodness or rightness) which does not derive from its consequences. The naïveté of consequentialist pacifism is clear from the fact that in the real world to abstain always and everywhere from using violence will be unreasonable. For it is sometimes necessary in order to protect ourselves and others from great harm. And against those who consider that pacifism is justified because the world would be a much better place if everyone refrained from violence we need only observe that we do not live in such a world.

This being so we must accept that there is some acceptable violence. But how are we to assess what is and what is not acceptable? Where do we draw the line? Clearly we are involved in an assessment of the importance of ends, the effectiveness and efficiency of means, and the certainty, or otherwise, of beliefs concerning them. If we are to use violence, we must be sure that our ends are worth the cost of achieving them by these means and that there are no other more acceptable means to the same ends. The costs and benefits involved are those of objective human goods and evils and not simply one's pet cause.

Though it is in principle possible to justify violence, it will clearly be very difficult in a political context. For political issues are amongst the most complex we face and there must be great risk attached to any violent approach to solutions to them. Perhaps we need not go so far as Hobbes, who argues that almost no violence could be justified because of the risk of the descent into the state of nature (a condition where there is a war of all against all and life is 'solitary, poor, nasty, brutish and short)'. The exception which Hobbes allows is where there is a direct threat to one's life. We could reasonably extend this somewhat to include any systematic denial of a basic human good where all other routes to an improvement have failed or are blocked.

However, before we may conclude that a revolution is

justified we must remember that there is the risk of great costs. To begin with, few revolutions succeed. The state has immensely powerful forces at its disposal so that even victory may be of the pyrrhic variety. Second, those which do succeed rarely fulfil their promise; they do not result in much of an improvement since they merely replace one élite with another. Third, the costs of violence and terror generally include those of creating a class of people who, through the use of these means, become hardened and vicious and who are likely to remain very dangerous indeed (to any regime). Fourth, it is clear that we have not exhausted all other means. Especially in those states possessed of some kind of democracy, the way is open, if not as open as it should be, to change through persuasion. This after all is the merit of such systems.

Is democracy special, then? It is often claimed that in a democratic system when a decision is taken according to the rules, no one is justified in breaking the rules (through violence or civil disobedience) in order to oppose the policy in question. Why, though, should this be so?

It may be said that democracy is the *correct and proper* system for policy making and therefore everyone is obliged (morally) to accept and observe the policy. As we have seen, however, the correctness of the system lies only in its tendency to serve certain ends. If the system goes against these ends with a certain policy wherein lie its merits?

A common response here is that it is unreasonable to break the law (properly arrived at) in any case because this undermines respect for law itself. Well clearly this is an overstatement. The law is broken with alarming frequency, yet respect for it remains stable. Further, it may well be worth risking this slippery slide into anarchy if our democracy adopts policies of terrible conse- quence. No principle outlaws pursuing the lesser of two evils.

Another proposed source of obligations of obedience is the consent of participants. In a democracy everyone (or everyone who is likely to go against policy illegally) participates and in so doing signals his acceptance of the system, creating expectations of *compliance* in his fellow participants. To renege thereafter is to reveal oneself as a fraud. There would be something in this argument if participation signalled an unconditional approval of the system. But it does not. We may merely signal our view that the system tends to produce reasonable policy and is therefore worth participating in. We do not concede that it is reasonable to accept its every dictate.

Thus we may conclude that there is no distinctively political obligation. Ultimate authority resides not in people, systems, law, or whatever, but in reasonableness (in the pursuit of good) itself. A person's only obligation is to be reasonable. This is not, however, to say that violence or civil disobedience is justified whenever the system produces unreasonable policies. That requires that the policies be very unreasonable and that no other means exist of changing them. Thus in a democracy illegal tactics will be harder to justify than elsewhere since there is usually the possibility of change, through elections or lobbying, for example.

Punishment

The practice of punishment is a severe problem for political philosophy, for if the purpose of the state is the good of its members (all of them) how can we punish some? Must punishment be good for them?

Some might think so. Since there will be a tendency, by a few all of the time and by many some of the time, to behave in ways which may ruin the lives of others and undermine the structure of the good society, a system of incentives (for cooperation) and disincentives (for non-cooperation) may be required. Punishment would be for extremely antisocial behaviour (that which offends against society's important rules – its laws). Since the life of crime is not the good life, a system which helps keep one on the straight and narrow is to be welcomed – by everyone. There is a tendency here to see punishment as educational or curative, to see criminals as irrational or ill. And in a good society, where each may enjoy all the basic goods, criminal behaviour would be one or the other, for it would be the pursuit of undesirable goals (goals not constitutive of the good life).

However, it may be denied that the good society will have criminals. Marx, for example, thought that in the future communist society individuals would pursue their interests only in socially constructive ways, and necessarily so since their self-development involves enjoying good social relations. This seems, however, to be wishful thinking.

Whatever the case, however, punishment does not seem to be a problem in the good society. In the good society criminal behaviour will always be unreasonable, so the reason for respecting someone's freedom is undermined. For criminality is the creation of bad social relations (of dishonesty, disrespect, violence, etc.), of such a serious sort that paternalism and the harm principle combine to sanction interference. The interference may be either preventative or educative; lock people up or reform them.

Now, for many this will not count as punishment because that practice requires the deliberate infliction of harm or suffering. And this will be done either as retribution or deterrence. What are we to make of such practices?

In the first place we must consider the problem of definition. Punishment, like any complex social institution, involves a complex of functions. It can be seen to have more than one end (which in itself is no criticism, since the good is a set of ends). Thus, for example, there are those who see punishment as primarily retributive; it simply pays back an offender for the wrong he has done. Again there are those who see punishment as a deterrent: its purpose is to discourage people from offending by imposing (the risk of) a heavy cost on so doing. Again there are those who see punishment as a form of treatment; it is educative or therapeutic, making the offender see the error of his ways. Most commonly people run these ideas together, something which will tend to confuse any attempt at justification.

The justification of the practice of punishment must relate to its real function. We must ask whether the purpose of punishment is or could be a good one, and if so, whether the benefits outweigh the costs. Further we must ask whether punishment is the best or only way to achieve this purpose.

It is clear that there will be breaches of society's rules and that we must respond in some way. Each of these purposes purports to explain why punishment is the proper response.

To see punishment as retribution is to see it as backward-looking. The offender has done something bad and therefore deserves to be punished. Thus there are two aspects here. The idea of deserving something and the idea that punishment is what is deserved. Desert here is treated as a primitive or underived notion. There just is a relation of desert between an offender and due punishment. This is another instance of what we called in Chapter 6 an *external* theory of justice (in this case retributive justice) and the same criticisms may be made. There simply is no direct link or relation between offending (or being evil) and being due a certain treatment. This is a corollary of there being no such relation between any characteristic (merit, labour) and a social right (reward or property, for example). Social forms mediate between these and social forms are to be assessed internally – that is with regard to the theory of the good alone. This is true of any system of justice.

If retribution cannot be given any such basis (if deontology is unreasonable) then it cannot be a good end for a system of punishment. If this is all punishment could rely on, it would fall prey to the accusations of institutionalized vengeance: it would be pointless and (because of the harm inflicted) evil.

The usual utilitarian defence of punishment sees its function as one of deterrence. If the deliberate infliction of disutility on some is outweighed by the utility produced by the prevention of offences (through discouragement) then the utilitarian accepts the value of punishment (if there is no other less costly means to this same end).

The trouble here is that once we define such a (desirable) end as deterring offences and accept that any efficient means to that end are justified, then we are opening the door, it would seem, to some extreme measures: for example, punishing innocent people, draconian punishment, torture, etc. These are to be allowed, the utilitarian admits, if they are economical deterrents.

Now, as argued in Chapter 1, it is not clear that utilitarianism does sanction such practices in any practicable social system. However, philosophers have devised imaginary cases and situations where such acts of deterrence would be justifiable on utilitarian grounds.

This means that the deterrence theory is one few of us could endorse – for an acceptable theory has to apply, acceptably, to all possible instances. In addition, however, we should note that utilitarianism seems to be giving the wrong reasons for not adopting these measures. The risk of social unease or breakdown is not the correct reason for not resorting to torture.

The utilitarian may not give up his deterrence theory at this point, however. For he may argue that although the deterrence theory does sanction using people, harming them, for the good of others, there are cases where we *must* accept this kind of thing and therefore his theory is on the right lines.

The kind of case in question is where normal human rights and decency are ignored in order to attain some great good or prevent a terrible catastrophe. For example, say the only way to save a city full of people is to torture, or threaten to kill, the man who has planted an atomic bomb, or those he cares for.

The strategy adopted in this chapter has been to try to develop an adequate political philosophy without resort to this kind of trade-off. That is, I have tried to justify a set of social practices to govern normal life on the basis of a theory of the good without using a theory which weighs one person's good against another, which will inflict suffering on some for the sake of some greater good. Such theories seem to me incoherent. Rawls has argued that all teleological theories fall into this way of thinking and so are to be rejected. I think this goes too far; it may be true of utilitarianism but it is not true of my approach, for I have explicitly excluded from the theory any point of view from which these judgements could be made.

By this I mean that there is no ideal observer nor any abstract homogeneous good that can be calculated over various options and used to determine the best one. We have got as far as we have by relying on the idea of a person's good requiring the good of others (through his need for social relations, for example). Interpersonal trade-off of welfare is beyond the scope of the theory and deliberately so.

This is not to say that the kind of moral problem described above is beyond answer. But the answer to it will come from the theory of ethics, and not from political philosophy, and will require more complex considerations than those employed by the utilitarian. It cannot be that the ethics of such questions reduces to an abstract calculation of utility. I shall not pursue this here, however, since the question at hand is punishment and the deterrence theory seems to entail that unacceptable means may be used *routinely*. This is surely much worse than allowing that they may be used to avert some catastrophe.

Thus the two major theories of punishment seem to fail. Are we to conclude, then, that punishment is unjustifiable? Perhaps not, but it is worth bearing in mind that the fact that a practice exists, and that we feel the need of it, does not mean that such a practice is necessarily justified.

The advantage of the retributive theory was that punishment was directed only to offenders. The advantage of the deterrence theory was that punishment was inflicted for a good end (though this, when pursued in utilitarian fashion, sanctioned more than punishment). Ideally we should like to combine both, that is, adopt a good end and limit ourselves to acceptable means in its pursuit. Some have tried to do just this by placing the notion of 'retribution in distribution' within the utilitarian framework of pursuing the end of deterrence.[10] That is, adopt the end of deterrence but forbid any other means to it but punishing the guilty.

This kind of approach fails, for once we have adopted the end of deterrence the rationality of any teleological approach dictates that we must accept whatever means to it are best. And this may not be punishment. And notice that we cannot rationally adopt ends which include, in their descriptions, the means to them – such as deterrence *by* retributive punishment. For this complex end merely conceals the real function of the practice (simple deterrence) which by itself is what gives the means to it value. Such an approach, then, gives only the appearance of resolving the problem by deliberately conflating distinct aspects of an acceptable justification. The utilitarian, by adopting this 'rule' utilitarian system, is trying to have his cake and eat it.

Still, the idea is nice. Could we find an acceptable end which restricts us to punishing only offenders to an acceptable degree? One possibility is the end of treatment. That is to say, we claim that in punishing we are treating people (for example, we may be 'teaching them a lesson'). In order to justify punishment in this way we have to show that in offending offenders are harming themselves and that punishment is a good way of 'curing' them.

Our analysis of the human good revealed that being unreasonably antisocial is a form of self-harm (it is to deny oneself a basic human good). Breaking a reasonable law, we can assume, is such a form of unreasonableness. And punishment is justified only if the laws are good ones.

As to whether punishment is a suitable treatment for offenders we may doubt. It seems to work best with non-human animals and children. Those who are set in their ways, for whom vice has become second nature, are less likely to respond to this kind of 'aversion therapy'. Perhaps there are other, better, treatments. However, punishment may still be fitting if, while not curing, it arrests the development of the vice. Imprisonment prevents the exercise of criminality and to that extent prevents self-harm. It is unlikely, however, that punishment can be given a blanket justification (to cover our present practices). More likely, punishment will have to be restricted to certain types of crime and certain types of criminal. And it is a matter of empirical research to discover whether and when punishment is a good form of treatment.

Reverse discrimination

Certain sections of the community have been, indeed still are, subject to unacceptable discrimination by the state (its laws and institutions), by employers and by individuals. To maintain a practice wherein certain people are discriminated against on grounds irrelevant to the activity concerned (for example, on grounds of sex, race, religion and social class) is bad because it is an expression of unacceptable social relationships and routinely uses people, usually against their will and always contrary to their good, to maintain bad social structures (of dominance, segregation and so on). Clearly such practices are to be got rid of.

However, what do we say of a practice which discriminates in favour of such people? That is to say, a practice which favours relevantly inferior people (inferior in terms of qualifications, experiences or potential) solely because they possess the correct 'irrelevant' characteristic? What would be the point of such reverse discrimination?

The idea seems to be that simply to get rid of unacceptable discrimination is not enough, at least in the short term. Reverse discrimination is needed either because the normal course is seen to be too slow at righting the situation (many of the disadvantaged may be dead before there is significant change) or because it is the only way of compensating people for the unacceptable disadvantages imposed on them by past circumstances, or both.

Each of these claims is contestable. If, for example, enough was done in the way of education, the transition to a more acceptable state of affairs might take only one or two generations. As for compensation, there might be better methods. Indeed there must be other methods, since many who have suffered are also, as a result, unable to benefit from reverse discrimination.

However, let us proceed on the assumption that reverse discrimination is the quickest route to a desirable end. That it is so is not a matter for the philosopher. Is it, however, a permissible means?

In the first place, it should be noted that reverse discrimination is not the mirror image of unfair discrimination, for an essential part of that is the use of an irrelevant characteristic as a basis of discrimination which maintains bad social relations and structures. If reverse discrimination is a useful means to the good society then it is using a now relevant characteristic to promote a good end. It cannot be said, then, that reverse discrimination is unacceptable in exactly the same way as unfair discrimination.

A second criticism is that reverse discrimination is unacceptable because it violates the rights of those who would normally have been successful if the practice were not in operation. What kind of right is this? The general idea seems to be this. In a fair system selection ought to proceed on the merit principle, that is, the post should go to the best-qualified applicant. The first thing to note is that this principle is not a matter of justice but a consideration of efficiency. We can see this from cases of 'over-qualification'. When someone is over-qualified for a post it may well be that they could perform better than anyone else in that post but it also seems perfectly fair to say that they should not get that post but should 'put their talents to better use' elsewhere. And this is because nothing is at stake apart from efficiency.

It may be said, however, that the operation of a merit system creates rights based on legitimate expectations that, say, this level of qualification is adequate for that particular post. To introduce reverse discrimination is to frustrate at least some expectations because some on the borderline will now fail (their places being taken by less well-qualified candidates). We may doubt how serious a consideration this frustration is, however. For if reverse discrimination is being operated properly it will generally favour those who would have been good enough to displace these candidates in any case (if they had not originally suffered as a result of unfair discrimination). However, though ignoring the merit principle is not a violation of any fundamental good, it does have its costs in terms of efficiency. It may be hoped, though, that in the long run this loss will be more than made up for by the more efficient use of the talents currently under-used through the operation of unfair practices.

It would seem, then, that there is no principled consideration which rules out reverse discrimination. It is something we may employ if it is an efficient means to the desirable end of a society characterized by good social relations. By the same token, however, there can be no principled consideration which makes reverse discrimination morally obligatory. This would only be so if it were the necessary form of compensation for past malpractice. However, it is not. As noted previously, the victims of such malpractice are not all in a position to benefit from reverse discrimination (for it may be that the harm done was so severe that an individual's potential is almost completely destroyed). Other forms of compensation are therefore required. And even if reverse discrimination is the best method in some cases, this will not be a matter of principle but a question of whether such a benefit is adequate in terms of its effects.

So we must turn to the question of whether or not reverse discrimination is an efficient means to our goal. This, we should note, is unlikely to have a very general answer. That is, the considerations adduced to produce an answer are likely to vary from society to society, and to vary in importance depending on the disadvantaged group at issue. For the appropriateness of this means will be a function of the severity of the original discrimination and the difficulties which the group in question faces in achieving parity.

It is clear, then, that to operate a practice of reverse discrimination is to conduct a social experiment. And one can only be certain of the success of an experiment in retrospect. However, it seems clear that there is a good case for conducting such an experiment, for while there may be short-term costs in terms of efficiency, the loss of self-esteem (indeed for some it will be an insult to be preferred on this basis) and perhaps a general undervaluing of any member of a disadvantaged group who is successful (with people thinking that they only succeed because it is made easier for them), the benefits promise to be large.

In the first place, to adopt a wait-and-see attitude concerning the effectiveness of a straightforward anti-discrimination policy may condemn many to a less good life than otherwise. For they need more in the way of encouragement than this. They need to see examples of their own kind in successful positions.

Second, discrimination may have been so bad that it has created deep-rooted hatred and resentment. Just to remove the causes of discrimination may not be enough to heal such social wounds. An act of real commitment, like reverse discrimination, will win many more friends immediately, and help to prevent any more serious breakdown of social relations.

Third, the sooner adequate numbers of such groups attain the desirable positions in society, the sooner we shall all come to accept and respect them. This is an enormous social benefit. Further, the best way to ensure that there is no real discrimination (and this happens despite laws to the contrary) is to ensure adequate representation of disadvantaged groups in positions of power (in hiring, legislating and so on). And it is to be hoped that we shall all benefit from this fresh perspective through its impact on social structures.

CONCLUSION

We have now seen a little of how political philosophy may work its way through into political practice. It has only been a little because issues of political practice are so complex that a whole book could easily be devoted to each one. However, the point of the exercise has been less to tell us how we should change the world than to discover what considerations are relevant to making changes for the better. Thus, as philosophers commonly say, the method developed matters more than any particular conclusion reached on the basis of that method. Of course, this is only to measure *philosophical* importance. If I am right, what matters most is the good life; the value of the present inquiry is to show us how we may argue about this and, more importantly in practice, how to develop the theory into a workable political philosophy.

NOTES

CHAPTER 1

1. Aristotle, *Nichomachean Ethics*, translated by W. D. Ross, OUP, 1925, I, vii, 1098a 17.
2. Sidgwick, H., *The Methods of Ethics*, Macmillan, 1901.
3. Rawls, J., *A Theory of Justice*, OUP, 1971.
4. Dworkin, R., 'Equality of Respect', *Philosophy and Public Affairs*, Fall 1981, p. 345.
5. See R. Nozick, *Anarchy, State and Utopia*, Blackwell, 1974, p. 223.

CHAPTER 2

1. Moore, G. E., *Principia Ethica*, CUP, 1903.
2. Rawls, J., *A Theory of Justice*, OUP, 1971, p. 22.
3. Dworkin, R., *Taking Rights Seriously*, Duckworth, 1977, chapters 9 and 12.
4. Bentham, J., *An Introduction to the Principles of Morals and Legislation*, Hafner, New York, 1970.
5. Mill, J. S., *Utilitarianism*, edited by Mary Warnock, Fontana, 1962.
6. ibid., p. 288.
7. ibid., p. 257.
8. ibid., p. 288.
9. *On Liberty* is also included in the above collection of Mill's work.
10. *Utilitarianism*, p. 293.
11. ibid., p. 292.
12. ibid., p. 289.
13. ibid., p. 289.
14. Sidgwick, H., *The Methods of Ethics*, Macmillan, 1901.

15. ibid., p. 98.
16. ibid., p. 127.
17. Singer, P., *Practical Ethics*, CUP, 1979, p. 12.
18. See, for example, R. M. Hare, *Moral Thinking*, OUP, 1981, chapter 6.
19. Singer, op. cit., p. 13.
20. Scanlon, T., 'Contractualism and Utilitarianism', in A. Sen and B. Williams, eds., *Utilitarianism and Beyond*, CUP, 1981.
21. ibid., p. 108.
22. ibid., p. 109–10.

CHAPTER 3
1. Rawls, J., *A Theory of Justice*, OUP, 1971, p. 3.
2. ibid., p. 30.
3. ibid., p. 62.
4. ibid., p. 11.
5. ibid., p. 248.
6. ibid., p. 139.
7. ibid., p. 126.
8. Williams, B., *Moral Luck*, CUP, 1981, p. 3 ('Persons, Character and Morality').
9. Rawls, op. cit., p. 184.
10. Smith, A., 'The Theory of the Moral Sentiments', in L. A. Selby-Bigge, *British Moralists*, OUP, 1897, vol. I, pp. 257–77.
11. Hume, D., *Treatise of Human Nature*, ed. L. A. Selby-Bigge, OUP, 1888, pp. 574–84.
12. Rawls, op. cit., p. 587.
13. ibid., p. 136.
14. ibid., p. 185.
15. ibid., p. 187.
16. ibid., p. 121.
17. Dworkin, R., 'Liberalism', in *Public and Private Morality*, ed. S. Hampshire, CUP, 1977, pp. 127ff.
18. ibid., p. 127.
19. Rawls, op. cit., p. 14.
20. ibid., p. 13.
21. ibid., p. 14.
22. Such arguments in favour of liberalism are offered by B. A. Ackerman, in *Social Justice in the Liberal State*, Yale University Press, 1980, chapters 10 and 11.
23. Rawls, op. cit., p. 31.
24. ibid., p. 396.
25. ibid., p. 433.

26. ibid., p. 328.
27. ibid., p. 527.
28. ibid., p. 527.
29. Rawls accepts this characterization in his 'Fairness to Goodness', *Philosophical Review*, 84 (1975), pp. 536–54.
30. Such an interpretation of Hume is offered by G. Harman, *The Nature of Morality*, OUP, 1977, and C. D. Broad, *Five Types of Ethical Theory*, Routledge & Kegan Paul, 1930.
31. Rawls, *A Theory of Justice*, p. 587.
32. ibid., p. 51.
33. Dworkin, R., *Taking Rights Seriously*, Duckworth, 1977, pp. 160ff.
34. ibid., p. 160.
35. ibid., p. 166.
36. MacIntyre, A., *After Virtue*, Duckworth, 1981.
37. Singer, P., 'Sidgwick and Reflective Equilibrium', *The Monist*, 58, pp. 490–517.
38. Rawls, *A Theory of Justice*, p. 21.
39. ibid., p. 21.
40. ibid., p. 256.
41. See, for example, I. Kant, *The Moral Law*, translated by H. J. Paton, Hutchinson, 1948, p. 67 (translation of *The Groundwork of the Metaphysics of Morals*).
42. Rawls, *A Theory of Justice*, p. 255.
43. ibid., p. 579.
44. ibid., p. 579.
45. ibid., p. 578.
46. ibid., p. 4.
47. For an example of the use of intuition or self-evidence in this way see J. Finnis, *Natural Law and Natural Rights*, OUP, 1980.
48. Rawls, *A Theory of Justice*, p. 27.
49. ibid., p. 416.
50. ibid., p. 28.
51. ibid., p. 328.
52. ibid., p. 328.
53. ibid., p. 329.
54. Ackerman, op. cit., p. 368.

CHAPTER 4
1. For the view that it cannot, see R. P. Wolff, *In Defense of Anarchism*, Harper & Row, 1970.
2. See, for example, T. Hobbes, *Leviathan*, edited by J. Plamenatz, Fontana, 1962.

3. See J. Locke, *The Second Treatise on Government*, in *Two Treatises on Government*, edited by P. Laslett, CUP, 1960.

4. Nozick, R., *Anarchy, State and Utopia*, Blackwell, 1974, p. 108.

5. Marx, K., *Capital*, edited by E. Mandel, Penguin Books, 1976, pp. 877 and 926.

6. Nozick, op. cit., p. 231.

7. ibid., p. 231.

8. ibid., p. 28.

9. ibid., p. ix.

10. MacIntyre, A., *After Virtue*, Duckworth, 1981, p. 67.

11. Nozick, R., *Philosophical Explanations*, OUP, 1981, p. 495.

12. Dworkin, R., *Taking Rights Seriously*, Duckworth, 1977, pp. 188–9.

13. ibid., pp. 272–3, for example.

14. Nozick, *Anarchy, State and Utopia*, p. 160.

15. Gewirth, A., *Reason and Morality*, Chicago University Press, 1978, p .171.

CHAPTER 5

1. Karl Marx, *Theses on Feuerbach*, 1845, XI.

2. 'Critique of the Gotha Program', in *Karl Marx: Selected Writings*, edited by D. McLellan, OUP, 1977, p. 569.

3. Cohen, G. A., *Karl Marx's Theory of History: a Defence*, OUP, 1978, p. ix.

CHAPTER 6

1. Mackie, J. L., *Ethics, Inventing Right and Wrong*, Penguin Books, 1977.

2. ibid., p. 59

3. ibid., p. 170.

4. ibid., p. 236.

5. ibid., p. 63.

6. Aristotle, *Nichomachean Ethics*, I, iii, 1094b 24.

7. Finnis, J., *Fundamentals of Ethics*, OUP, 1983, p. 76.

8. Williams, B., *Morality*, CUP, 1972, p. 76.

9. Hardie, W. F. R., *Aristotle's Ethical Theory*, OUP, 1968, p. 23.

10. Williams, *Morality*, p. 74.

11. Mackie, op. cit., p. 47.

12. Clark, S. R. L., *The Nature of the Beast*, OUP, 1982, p. 101.

13. Williams, *Morality*, p. 68.

14. Rawls, *A Theory of Justice*, p. 578.

15. Berlin, I., 'Two Concepts of Liberty', in his *Four Essays on Liberty*, OUP, 1969.

16. Williams, B., 'Conflicts of Values', in his *Moral Luck*, CUP, 1981.
17. Berlin, *Four Essays on Liberty*, p. 169.
18. Cf. Aristotle, *Nichomachean Ethics*, IX, x.

CHAPTER 7

 1. Cf. Rescher, N., *Distributive Justice*, Bobbs-Merrill, 1966, chapter
    1.
 2. Karl Marx, *Karl Marx: Selected Writings*, edited by D. McLellan,
    OUP, 1977, p. 238.
 3. Cf. Rawls, *A Theory of Justice*, pp. 126ff.
 4. Finnis, J., *Natural Law and Natural Rights*, OUP, 1980, p. 86.
 5. ibid., p. 86.
 6. *Nichomachean Ethics*, IX, ix, 1170a 23.
 7. Mill, J. S., *The Principles of Political Economy*, Kelley, 1976,
    p. 760n.
 8. Popper, K., *The Open Society and Its Enemies*, Routledge & Kegan
    Paul, 1945.
 9. Honderich, T., *Violence for Equality*, Penguin Books, 1980, p. 152.
10. Cf. Rawls, J., 'Two Concepts of Rules', *Philosophical Review*,
    1955.

FURTHER READING

CHAPTER I

General introductions to the subject include:

Feinberg, J., *Social Philosophy*, Prentice Hall, 1973.

Pettit, P., *Judging Justice*, Routledge & Kegan Paul, 1980.

Raphael, D. D., *Problems of Political Philosophy*, Macmillan, 1976.

Some useful discussions of issues raised in this chapter are:

Ackerman, B. A., *Social Justice in the Liberal State*, Yale University Press, 1980, Part 4.

Galston, W. A., *Justice and the Human Good*, University of Chicago Press, 1980, chapter 2.

Nielsen, K., *Equality and Liberty*, Rowman & Allenhead, 1985, Part 1.

Nozick, R., *Anarchy, State, and Utopia*, Blackwell, 1974, chapter 1.

Plamenatz, J., 'The Use of Political Theory' in *Political Philosophy*, edited by A. Quinton, OUP, 1967.

Rawls, J., *A Theory of Justice*, OUP, 1971, sections 1, 9, 20, 69, 87.

CHAPTER 2

The views discussed in this chapter are derived from these works:

Bentham, J., *The Principles of Morals and Legislation*, Hafner, 1970.

Mill, J. S., *Utilitarianism*, edited by Mary Warnock, Fontana, 1962.

Sidgwick, H., *The Methods of Ethics*, Macmillan, 1901.

Singer, P., *Practical Ethics*, CUP, 1979.

Scanlon, T., 'Contractualism and Utilitarianism', in *Utilitarianism and Beyond*, edited by A. Sen and B. Williams, CUP, 1981.

Critical works on utilitarianism include:

Mackie, J. L., *Ethics*, Penguin Books, 1977.
Plamenatz, J., *The English Utilitarians*, Blackwell, 1958 – which
    generously includes a chapter on David Hume.
Quinton, A., *Utilitarian Ethics*, Macmillan, 1973.
Smart, J. J. C., and Williams, B., *Utilitarianism: For and Against*,
    CUP, 1973.

For modern proponents of distinctive utilitarian views see:
Brandt, R. B., *A Theory of the Good and the Right*, OUP, 1979.
Hare, R. M., *Moral Thinking*, OUP, 1981.
Regan, D. H., *Utilitarianism and Co-operation*, OUP, 1980.

CHAPTER 3
Barry, B., *The Liberal Theory of Justice*, OUP, 1973.
Blocker, H. G., and Smith, E. H., eds., *John Rawls' Theory of Social
    Justice*, Ohio University Press, 1980.
Daniels, N., *Reading Rawls*, Blackwell, 1975.
Dworkin, R., *Taking Rights Seriously*, Duckworth, 1977, chapter 6.
    'Liberalism' in *Public and Private Morality*, edited by S.
    Hampshire, CUP, 1977.
Sandel, M. J., *Liberalism and the Limits of Justice*, CUP, 1982.
Wolff, R. P., *Understanding Rawls*, Princeton University Press, 1977.

CHAPTER 4
On libertarian thought generally see:
Friedman, M. and R., *Free to Choose*, Secker & Warberg, 1980.
Hayek, F., *The Constitution of Liberty*, Routledge & Kegan Paul, 1960.
Machin, T. R., *The Libertarian Reader*, Rowman & Littlefield, 1982.

On Nozick see:
Barber, B., 'Deconstituting Politics', in M. Freedman and D.
    Robertson, eds., *The Frontiers of Political Theory*, Harvester,
    1980.
Norman, R., 'Does Equality Destroy Liberty', in *Contemporary
    Political Philosophy*, edited by K. Graham, CUP, 1982.
Sandel, M. J., *Liberalism and the Limits of Justice*, CUP, 1982.

On rights:
Becker, L., *Property Rights*, Routledge & Kegan Paul, 1977.
Dworkin, R., *Taking Rights Seriously*, Duckworth, 1977.
Gewirth, A., *Reason and Morality*, University of Chicago Press, 1980.
Pennock, J. R., and Chapman, J. W., eds., *Human Rights*, New York
    University Press, 1981.

CHAPTER 5

Good sources for the writings of Marx are:
McLellan, D., ed., *Karl Marx: Selected Writings*, OUP, 1977,
Tucker, R., *The Marx/Engels Reader*, Norton, 1972.

Worthwhile critical works include:
Cohen, G. A., *Karl Marx's Theory of History: A Defence*, OUP, 1978.
Elster, J., *Making Sense of Marx*, CUP, 1985.
Lukes, S., *Marxism and Morality*, OUP, 1985.
Plamenatz, J., *Karl Marx's Philosophy of Man*, OUP, 1975.
Singer, P., *Marx*, OUP, 1980.

CHAPTER 6

Aristotle, 'Ethics' and 'Politics', in *The Basic Works of Aristotle*, edited
    by R. McKeon, Random House, 1941.
Bambrough, R., *Moral Knowledge and Moral Scepticism*, Routledge &
    Kegal Paul, 1979.
Clark, S. R. L., *Artistotle's Man*, OUP, 1975.
Finnis, J., *Natural Law and Natural Rights*, OUP, 1980.
    Fundamentals of Ethics, OUP, 1983.
Galston, W. A., *Justice and the Human Good*, University of Chicago
    Press, 1980.
Hardie, W. F. R., *Aristotle's Ethical Theory*, OUP, 1968.
Mackie, J. L., *Ethics*, Penguin Books, 1977.
Midgley, M., *Beast and Man*, Harvester, 1979.
Trigg, R., *The Shaping of Man*, Blackwell, 1982.
Williams, B., *Ethics and the Limits of Philosophy*, Fontana, 1985.

CHAPTER 7

Braverman, H., *Labor and Monopoly Capital*, Monthly Review Press,
    1974.
Cohen, M., and others, eds., *Equality and Preferential Treatment*,
    Princeton University Press, 1977.
Harris, J., *The Value of Life*, Routledge & Kegan Paul, 1985.
    Violence and Responsibility, Routledge & Kegan Paul, 1980.
Honderich, Ted, *Punishment*, Penguin Books, 1971.
    Violence for Equality, Penguin Books, 1980.
Ignatiev, M., *The Needs of Strangers*, Chatto & Windus, 1981.
Nelson, W. N., *On Justifying Democracy*, Routledge & Kegan Paul,
    1980.

INDEX

FOR THE BEST IN PAPERBACKS, LOOK FOR THE 🐧

PENGUIN HISTORY

The Germans   Gordon A. Craig

An intimate study of a complex and fascinating nation by 'one of the ablest and most distinguished American historians of modern Germany' – Hugh Trevor-Roper

Imperial Spain 1469–1716   J. H. Elliot

A brilliant modern study of the sudden rise of a barren and isolated country to the greatest power on earth, and of its equally sudden decline. 'Outstandingly good' – *Daily Telegraph*

British Society 1914–1945   John Stevenson

A major contribution to the *Penguin Social History of Britain*, which 'will undoubtedly be the standard work for students of modern Britain for many years to come' – *The Times Educational Supplement*

A History of Christianity   Paul Johnson

'Masterly ... It is a huge and crowded canvas – a tremendous theme running through twenty centuries of history – a cosmic soap opera involving kings and beggars, philosophers and crackpots, scholars and illiterate *exaltés*, popes and pilgrims and wild anchorites in the wilderness' – Malcolm Muggeridge

The Penguin History of Greece   A. R. Burn

Readable, erudite, enthusiastic and balanced, this one-volume history of Hellas sweeps the reader along from the days of Mycenae and the splendours of Athens to the conquests of Alexander and the final dark decades.

A History of Latin America   George Pendle

'Ought to be compulsory reading in every sixth form ... this book is right on target' – *Sunday Times*. 'A beginner's guide to the continent ... lively, and full of anecdote' – *Financial Times*

The Penguin History of the United States   Hugh Brogan

'An extraordinarily engaging book' – *The Times Literary Supplement*.
'Compelling reading ... Hugh Brogan's book will delight the general
reader as much as the student' – *The Times Educational Supplement*. 'He
will be welcomed by American readers no less than those in his own
country' – J. K. Galbraith

The Making of the English Working Class   E. P. Thompson

Probably the most imaginative – and the most famous – post-war work of
English social history.

The Waning of the Middle Ages   Johan Huizinga

A magnificent study of life, thought and art in 14th- and 15th-century
France and the Netherlands, long established as a classic.

The City in History   Lewis Mumford

Often prophetic in tone and containing a wealth of photographs, *The City
in History* is among the most deeply learned and warmly human studies of
man as a social creature.

The Habsburg Monarchy 1809–1918   A. J. P. Taylor

Dissolved in 1918, the Habsburg Empire 'had a unique character, out of
time and out of place'. Scholarly and vividly accessible, this 'very good
book indeed' (*Spectator*) elucidates the problems always inherent in the
attempt to give peace, stability and a common loyalty to a heterogeneous
population.

Inside Nazi Germany   Conformity, Opposition and Racism in Everyday Life
Detlev J. K. Peukert

An authoritative study – and a challenging and original analysis – of the
realities of daily existence under the Third Reich. 'A fascinating study ...
captures the whole range of popular attitudes and the complexity of their
relationship with the Nazi state' – Richard Geary

PENGUIN HISTORY

The Victorian Underworld Kellow Chesney

A superbly evocative survey of the vast substratum of vice that lay below the respectable surface of Victorian England – the showmen, religious fakes, pickpockets and prostitutes – and of the penal methods of that 'most enlightened age'. 'Charged with nightmare detail' – *Sunday Times*

A History of Modern France Alfred Cobban

Professor Cobban's renowned three-volume history, skilfully steering the reader through France's political and social problems from 1715 to the Third Republic, remains essential reading for anyone wishing to understand the development of a great European nation.

Stalin Isaac Deutscher

'The Greatest Genius in History' and the 'Life-Giving Force of Socialism'? Or a tyrant more ruthless than Ivan the Terrible whose policies facilitated the rise of Nazism? An outstanding biographical study of a revolutionary despot by a great historian.

Montaillou Cathars and Catholics in a French Village 1294–1324
Emmanuel Le Roy Ladurie

'A classic adventure in eavesdropping across time' – Michael Ratcliffe in *The Times*

The Second World War A. J. P. Taylor

A brilliant and detailed illustrated history, enlivened by all Professor Taylor's customary iconaclasm and wit.

Industry and Empire E. J. Hobsbawm

Volume 3 of the *Penguin Economic History of Britain* covers the period of the Industrial Revolution: 'the most fundamental transformation in the history of the world recorded in written documents.' 'A book that attracts and deserves attention ... by far the most gifted historian now writing' – John Vaizey in the *Listener*

Political Ideas   David Thomson (ed.)

From Machiavelli to Marx – a stimulating and informative introduction to the last 500 years of European political thinkers and political thought.

On Revolution   Hannah Arendt

Arendt's classic analysis of a relatively recent political phenomenon examines the underlying principles common to all revolutions, and the evolution of revolutionary theory and practice. 'Never dull, enormously erudite, always imaginative' – *Sunday Times*

The Apartheid Handbook   Roger Omond

The facts behind the headlines: the essential hard information about how apartheid actually works from day to day.

The Social Construction of Reality   Peter Berger and Thomas Luckmann

Concerned with the sociology of 'everything that passes for knowledge in society' and particularly with that which passes for common sense, this is 'a serious, open-minded book, upon a serious subject' – *Listener*

The Care of the Self   Michel Foucault
The History of Sexuality Vol 3

Foucault examines the transformation of sexual discourse from the Hellenistic to the Roman world in an inquiry which 'bristles with provocative insights into the tangled liaison of sex and self' – *The Times Higher Educational Supplement*

A Fate Worse than Debt   Susan George

How did Third World countries accumulate a staggering trillion dollars' worth of debt? Who really shoulders the burden of reimbursement? How should we deal with the debt crisis? Susan George answers these questions with the solid evidence and verve familiar to readers of *How the Other Half Dies*.

I: The Philosophy and Psychology of Personal Identity   Jonathan Glover

From cases of split brains and multiple personalities to the importance of memory and recognition by others, the author of *Causing Death and Saving Lives* tackles the vexed questions of personal identity. 'Fascinating … the ideas which Glover pours forth in profusion deserve more detailed consideration' – Anthony Storr

Minds, Brains and Science   John Searle

Based on Professor Searle's acclaimed series of Reith Lectures, *Minds, Brains and Science* is 'punchy and engaging … a timely exposé of those woolly-minded computer-lovers who believe that computers can think, and indeed that the human mind is just a biological computer' – *The Times Literary Supplement*

Ethics   Inventing Right and Wrong   J. L. Mackie

Widely used as a text, Mackie's complete and clear treatise on moral theory deals with the status and content of ethics, sketches a practical moral system and examines the frontiers at which ethics touches psychology, theology, law and politics.

The Penguin History of Western Philosophy   D. W. Hamlyn

'Well-crafted and readable … neither laden with footnotes nor weighed down with technical language … a general guide to three millennia of philosophizing in the West' – *The Times Literary Supplement*

Science and Philosophy: Past and Present   Derek Gjertsen

Philosophy and science, once intimately connected, are today often seen as widely different disciplines. Ranging from Aristotle to Einstein, from quantum theory to renaissance magic, Confucius and parapsychology, this penetrating and original study shows such a view to be both naive and ill-informed.

The Problem of Knowledge   A. J. Ayer

How do you *know* that this is a book? How do you *know* that you know? In *The Problem of Knowledge* A. J. Ayer presented the sceptic's arguments as forcefully as possible, investigating the extent to which they can be met. 'Thorough … penetrating, vigorous … readable and manageable' – *Spectator*